Back *and* Forth

Back *and* Forth

Using an EDITOR'S MINDSET to Improve Student Writing

LEE HEFFERNAN

Foreword by ROZLYN LINDER

I like the new lead. Catches my attention right off!

Original!

Let me know what you think about my suggestions.

Powerful theme!

Let's talk more about transitions.

Can this be expanded?

Perfect for our classroom press!

You found and fixed your spelling errors. Way to go!

Get going on revisions! We can't wait to publish!

HEINEMANN
Portsmouth, NH

Heinemann
361 Hanover Street
Portsmouth, NH 03801–3912
www.heinemann.com

Offices and agents throughout the world

The author and publisher wish to thank those who have generously given permission to reprint borrowed material:

Figure 2.2: From "Meet the Latest Newbery Winner: How Katherine Applegate Created a Modern-Day Classic" by Elizabeth Bird in *School Library Journal*, posted March 3, 2013. Copyright © 2017 by *School Library Journal*. Used by permission of the publisher. www.slj.com/2013/03/interviews/the-one-and-only-how-Katherine-applegate-created-a-classic-and-nabbed-the-newbery/.

Cataloging-in-Publication Data is on file with the Library of Congress.
ISBN: 978-0-325-08982-9

Editor: Holly Kim Price
Production: Vicki Kasabian
Interior and cover designs: Suzanne Heiser
Typesetter: Kim Arney
Manufacturing: Steve Bernier

Printed in the United States of America on acid-free paper
21 20 19 18 17   VP   1 2 3 4 5

For my true-blue crew: Peter, Rosalyn, and Quinn
And for my parents, Ann and Dan

CONTENTS

FOREWORD

Guilty as charged. I can recall numerous times when I asked a student, "Are you ready to publish your writing?" I swiftly sent them off to rewrite, type, or illustrate their work. That writing was then retired to a class bulletin board, or even worse— my desk. Done. That was the end of that piece. It now belonged to me. Lee Heffernan has shown me the error of my ways.

Lee's book speaks to the idea of student empowerment, accountability, meaningful writing, revision, and publishing. Her work essentially shows us how to move students from _fake_ writing (writing that is just for the teacher) to writing that has purpose and passion. Lee manages to marry process and product in a way that will inevitably set a new standard for writing instruction for teachers everywhere. Her work breaks ground with tenets that shift our writing instructional norms and inspires students.

Lee introduces her students to a three-tiered small press publishing model. Students learn about the authentic goals of publishing: fostering relationships, connecting to readers, and revising to improve text. But she doesn't just stop there. The class creates a student press by deciding the type of writing that they want to do, designing the logo, and, as important, delving into the roles of both editors and writers.

She suggests that students identify and study some of their favorite books, examining who the publishers are and learning the recursive process of writing and revision. Revision and ownership are at the heart of writing and Heffernan makes that clear and exciting! What _actually_ happens when professional editors and writers work? What is the role of authentic revision? In this book, Heffernan brings the notion of _authentic_ purposes for writing by putting students in the role of author.

At the heart of her model are collaboration and revision. Students learn to collaborate and work together to offer one another feedback. Lee gets students to understand the actual value of multiple revisions. After working with fellow student–authors, students learn how to prepare their writing for submission to the classroom press.

Student-created small presses? Student investment in revision? The moment I dove into this book, I was in awe. Heffernan has created a model for writing instruction that is transformative in how students can view their work as professional and authentic.

As I read Lee's book, page by page, like a favorite novel, I found it hard to tear myself away. It is impossible to read this book and not get chills up your spine about the possibilities for building writers who not only love their craft, but understand the role of professional editors and writers. With every page turn, I wanted to know more, see more, and soak in each student sample. The student enthusiasm jumps off the page and you can feel the excitement and ownership of the classroom presses that are featured in this book. Students begin to see themselves just like professional writers—with a genuine purpose. That repositioning of writing is amazing and powerful. This model has transformed the way I think of student ownership, revision, and publication. Lee Heffernan takes something as intriguing and exciting as authentic writing and makes it fun to implement for students and teachers.

—Rozlyn Linder

ACKNOWLEDGMENTS

Thank you, Peter Sternberg, for reading every draft and cheering me on every step of the way. Without you, Husbandman, we both know this book would not exist.

Thank you to my two fabulous families—the Heffernans and the Rumpf-Sternbergs.

Thank you to friends and cheerleaders Judith Williams, KC West, Nancy Reynolds, Kathy Vanderschans, Sandra Lewis, Jayma Acton, Mary Sudbury, Karen Adams, Cynthia Butler, Janet Cowperthwaite, and so many wonderful others.

Thank you to Mitzi Lewison, friend and thesis advisor, for years of fun and fascinating collaborations in and out of my classroom.

Thanks to Ursula Nordstrom for inspiration from the very beginning. And many thanks to my friend, Dorothy Menosky, the dear genius who first shared Ursula's work with me way back when.

Thank you to my amazing editor, Holly Kim Price. I'm forever grateful to you for your insights and advice that helped shape each chapter of this book as we passed it back and forth on its journey from Indiana University dissertation to Heinemann publication.

Finally, thanks to all the creative and compassionate authors who publish with Popcorn Press. You inspire me every day to publish books that POP!

INTRODUCTION

One Sunday morning, I was relishing some time with coffee and the newspaper when I came across an article that took my mind straight into my classroom. The article was about one of my favorite authors, Roald Dahl, and his work with his editors. Dahl had a reputation among editors for being difficult when it came to revising his texts. Just that week I had worked with quite a few young writers who I might describe as a wee bit difficult when it came to revising. I thought about my inability to help students who didn't want to make changes to their texts. I also reflected on my concern about students who simply jotted down the first revision that came to mind so they could move on to the next step in their writing process.

The article about Dahl piqued my interest. It surprised me to hear that his editors requested changes to his manuscripts. I wondered, "How much revision would Roald Dahl really need to have to do? He's Roald Dahl!" It turns out this famous author actually had to do a great deal of revising before his books were published and he had guidance and support with his revisions from several editors over the course of his career.

What did Dahl's editors know that I didn't know? Why was it so difficult to get my students to make even minor revisions? Where Dahl's editors were asking for passage rewrites and chapter deletions, I was asking about small changes, an added detail here or a bit of dialogue there. Though Dahl and his editors sometimes argued about revisions, his books were revised extensively as Dahl and his editors passed his manuscripts back and forth over long periods of time. The description of Dahl's involvement with his editors made me wonder, *How could I engage my students more effectively in a process of revision? How could I become more of a partner to them as we worked to publish their writing?*

My Years as a "Fellow Writer" in the Writing Workshop

I began my teaching career thoroughly committed to writing process pedagogy. Like any teacher, my goal was to help students become better writers, as they developed their ideas and eventually published their drafts. Process writing allowed students in my classrooms to make creative choices. Personal interests were the foundation of their topic selections and students felt they were in charge of their publications. Process writing also brought an authenticity to the writing curriculum. A first draft was no longer considered a final copy, simply handed in to the teacher to be graded and returned. It now represented a student's attempt to document and explore thoughts and questions about the world. Writing workshop was and is a favorite time of day for me and for my students: a social, productive time, with students writing, sharing their pieces, conferring together, and illustrating final copies.

Writing process research encouraged teachers to become writers along with their students. I took up this role with gusto, using my own writing products and processes to model and demonstrate elements of drafting, revising, and editing. I joined a writer's group, read a plethora of professional books about teaching writ-

ing, attended professional conferences, and filled up one notebook after another. As a fellow writer, I was careful to respect student control of their texts during writing conferences.

Teacher friends who did not consider themselves to be writers often expressed insecurity about their proficiency as writing teachers. Many times colleagues would say, "You like to write, Lee. I don't. That's why you can teach writing and I can't." Although being a fellow writer in the workshop felt comfortable to me, this identity could also be problematic as I tried to spend time on my writing and keep up with the demands of classroom teaching. Lucy Calkins acknowledged the difficulty of performing the dual roles of teacher and writer in a conference presentation when she jokingly told the story of a teacher who shares the same draft year after year with students, acting as if she wrote it the night before. Everyone in attendance could relate to this story. I had taken such practical shortcuts myself.

Even though I identified as a writer, I gradually got the sense that my being a writer was not having a profound impact on student writing. Over the years, I found myself reading stacks of same old same old kind of writing. Students took their texts through a writing process, from idea to final copy, but many tended to write repetitively on recycled topics that weren't new to them. My enthusiasm for writing time flagged a bit after years of reading the same types of stories over and over again—stories about baseball games, family pets, sleepovers. I groaned when students told me they wanted to write fiction because I struggled to maintain interest in these retellings of favorite video games or popular television shows.

In our writing conferences, we rarely discussed significant revision possibilities even though I knew revision was essential to the writing process. As a fellow writer, I hesitated to make suggestions that would change the direction of their pieces. Students picked up on my hesitance and registered ambivalence about making changes to their texts. I could not seem to strike a balance between honoring their independence as fellow writers and assisting with the hard work of rewriting

and revising. I was not able to communicate the importance of revision, no matter how I tried via minilessons, conferences, and demonstrations. Students often ended up publishing final drafts that were only slightly different from their original rough drafts.

Lack of substantive revision is not a problem specific to my classroom, but is common in many schools. Haar and Horning find "student writers are more likely to stick to surface correction and small changes" when it comes to revising, even at the secondary level (2006, 4). Although process writing teachers know the importance of revision, we're not always sure about *how* to help students rewrite. We're told to ask questions in our conferences, but what should we do when our questions don't seem to lead students to revise their texts? Is it OK to make suggestions? If so, should we be direct with our suggestions? How direct? What if the writer doesn't care for our ideas? Should we push our point if we believe the text needs improvements, or should we respect student ownership of text and leave well enough alone?

My hesitation in the revision process stood in stark contrast to the ways editors work with published authors. When I found the article about Roald Dahl, I sensed that there was something to author and editor work that could be helpful for me as a writing teacher. I talked about the article with Judith Williams, our school's media specialist, who shared with me a biography of Tomie dePaola (Elleman 1999). The biography showed samples of how dePaola and a range of people at

his publishing house work on revisions. I used photographs from Elleman's book to show students examples of what extensive revision could look like. I was intrigued by the description of dePaola's relationship with his longtime editor. Margaret Frith had a hand in the creation of dePaola's books, not on a mere conventions level, but on a conceptual level as well. Although I, like many people, had always imagined *proofreader* when I heard the word *editor*, dePaola's editor worked intensively with him to revise, often making contributions that changed a story's direction. Frith and dePaola's work together involved intense negotiation around the substance of his manuscripts, which at times meant winning or losing arguments about content, resulting in unpleasant tensions as well as satisfying resolutions. Their work together spanned over three decades.

As I learned more about editors, I became bolder about interacting with writers during the revision process. My students and I became "textworkers," treating their texts like clay, shaping them to influence readers (Kamler 2001; Heffernan 2004). We were already having rich discussions about important topics in reading workshop and now I wanted writing workshop to also be a time for powerful conversations. I began to look for ways to bring more social purpose to student writing, encouraging students to write on more critical or social themes that mattered to them.

Though I knew that revision could provide opportunities for helping students enact social goals in their writing (Welch 1997), I sometimes worried about my new, more directive, role in revision work. Was I too involved? Was I crossing some kind of line in this work with young writers? I turned to editor literature not to learn about a set procedure for editing but to gather information about multiple ways editors help writers while respecting their authorship.

Focusing on Product, as Well as Process

By focusing on the writing process, I aimed to help writers improve their writing skills. By focusing more on product, editors are freed of this pressure. They don't need to work to help the writer improve their writing skills, to write a better book in the future. Although editors don't attend to writing process, they do revise with writers. Each writing project is unique and changes with each writer and with each book. Editors must home in on product over process because the stakes of the

work are high, particularly for small presses. If they don't sell books, they go out of business. I continue to work on helping students develop their writing processes, but learning more about editors has increased my focus on product because publishing means more to me than it used to.

I wondered why I hadn't learned more about editor–author relationships in all my professional reading and inquiry about writing workshop. Publishing is usually the goal of process writing, but there's not much written about how teachers can emulate the work of editors. I learned from editor Gerald Gross that the work of the editor is usually invisible to readers and some may even say the work is kept "in the closet" (1993, xvi). Editorial contributions to texts are usually not widely acknowledged because the work of the editor disappears when a text is published. Although the author owns the text before *and after* the publishing process, editor and author share it during the path from manuscript to published book. Writing researcher Timothy Lensmire claims that a focus on individuality and authenticity is present in writing classrooms. Even as we recognize the social nature of reading and writing, we idealize the image of the individual writer as a solitary artist, working alone (2000, 16–17). In *Editors on Editing* (1993), Gross pushes for more openness about the work that editors do with authors:

> I would like to propose a revolutionary way of recognizing the midwifery of the editor. Since at least the legendary Maxwell Perkins's time, editors have been expected to be unsung, faceless, nameless technicians assisting the author in the creation of the completed manuscript. Quite often, of course, the author graciously and gratefully acknowledges the efforts of his or her editor in the prefatory pages of the published book. Quite often, though the editor remains unsung. But why does it always have to be that way? More important, why should it be that way? (xvi)

I'm grateful to the many authors and editors who came "out of the closet" to share information and guidelines about their publishing journeys. Editors who have talked and written about the ways they work have provided criteria for my own work as an editor in the classroom publishing house. From a review of literature by and about editors, I've learned that editors are guided in their work by a sense of responsibility to relationship, text, and readership.

Although there's no one set way that editors work with writers, these three responsibilities, or commitments, are helpful guidelines. If you find yourself wishing that your work with student writers could lead to more intentionality about revising and publishing texts that change during the writing process, improving from one draft to the next, you too may want to reconsider your role in writing workshop. As classroom editors, we keep the following commitments in mind:

- Relationship: In the working relationship of the writer and the editor, the writer does not lack agency, but the editor is in a greater position of power and so bears greater responsibility for making the relationship positive and productive. Neither editor nor writer benefits if the relationship sours and does not result in a publication.

- Text: An editor's job is to make suggestions that will lead to an improved text. Editors respect that the writer owns the text while expecting that the text is going to change during its journey through the publishing house and into the hands of readers. Editors are committed to the job of making suggestions that lead to improvements in texts.

- Readership: Editors keep in mind the world of the reader, and their decisions are inevitably influenced by ideas about future readers of their publications. Before accepting a manuscript, an editor must analyze a text to determine if it fits with the goals of their publishing house. Publishers release a limited number of books every year, so each book is important. Though large publishing firms tend to have lists that are more eclectic, some smaller presses tailor their lists to specific purposes.

These three commitments have helped me in my work with students. When I work with student writers, I take care to keep the writing relationship productive and respectful. I advocate for their texts and work, helping students to enact changes through revision to make the text the best it can be. I keep in mind that these texts are being written for readers who are looking for books that are fresh, original, and creative. Keeping in mind that my students are writing for readers, and not just for themselves, I consider ways to help students match their writing purposes with their intended audience.

An Editor's Frame of Mind in the Classroom Press

I have never stopped believing in the importance of a writing workshop approach to teaching writing, but over the years, I have shifted my role in the workshop. Although I still act as a fellow writer when teaching students about finding and developing topics, I now take up the role of classroom press editor when students work on drafts that they want to publish. Our classroom has become a small press where students, with the help of their editor, work to revise manuscripts in substantive ways before they're published. Creating a small press in our classroom involves a shift of perspective. We've always published student work in our writing workshops. With a small press model, students now work with their teacher–editor to reimagine and reshape their drafts more purposefully. This shift in writing workshop brings classroom publishing a step closer to what actually happens when professional writers publish.

Small press publishing takes more time than is perhaps typical for your writing workshop. Substantive revision is more time-consuming for both teacher and student. Because of this, it's important to ease into the model and make it your own. With a classroom press, publishing slows down and students delve more deeply into the writing process, with the help of their editor. As the editor of the classroom press, the teacher decides which pieces are published through the press and which are not. There's no set protocol, and small presses are unique in their creative visions and goals.

Although the basic format of writing workshop remains consistent with a small press model, the teacher's mindset shifts as we experiment with a more interactive approach to revision. During the school year, we will choose which writing projects will be published with the press. Not all writing projects must involve the back-and-forth negotiation between the teacher–editor and the student-author. Teachers can make decisions about which pieces will become classroom press publications and which will continue to be part of the established curricular grade level goals.

In addition to keeping writer's notebooks, students work on independent DIY publications during writing workshop when they're not involved with a classroom project. Students will come to distinguish between the classroom press projects and the more independent, DIY publishing projects they complete using simple book-making materials available in the classroom. These independent books are posted in the writing center and are student driven. Just as we wouldn't go through our students' writer's notebooks and grade their individual pieces, the DIY books are not assessed with formal grades, but do give us information about our students' writing identities. This independent writing not only helps to build writing stamina and identity but also serves to increase student awareness about self-publishing, which is an avenue that more and more writers are taking advantage of today.

I like to assure students that if they're working on something that's very important to them, but that's not quite in line with the goals of our classroom press, I am happy to read it over and give them feedback. Books that are published by the classroom press, however, will be the product of work that has gone through the back-and-forth editing process. During this process, students revise their drafts several times and for different purposes. No student publishes until their text is the best it can be. As I work with students, I'm helping them revise the conventions, meanings, craft, and purposes of their pieces. If a piece has been published with the press, it's of high quality and student formal evaluations, or grades, will reflect their growth as writers through the revision process. Being an editor for students is a shift in thinking about the teacher's role in the writing workshop and is adaptable to your curricular goals.

With a classroom press model, younger students start acquiring the skills that they will need in the upper grades. The work of authors and their editors provides models for helping students develop their skills as producers and distributors of texts. Throughout this book, I review writing research about revising and publishing student texts. Along the way, I also explore the various ways editors work with authors and share how an editor's frame of mind can be applied to writing workshops in our classrooms. Drawing on literature about writing as well as publishing, I introduce ways that a teacher-as-editor model can help

us shift our ways of thinking about texts. As teacher–editors, we can be more involved with revision and give our students the kind of guidance that resembles what editors do for and with professional writers.

In the following chapters, I explore what I've learned about how writing research supports a teacher-as-editor frame of mind in the writing workshop:

- Chapter 1, "Introducing a Small Press Publishing Model to Student Writers": Before becoming an editor for students, we need to build student knowledge base about the ins and outs of the world of publishing.

- Chapter 2, "Fostering Relationships: Keeping Revision Work Positive and Productive": As classroom editors, we can use a range of strategies for building trusting relationships with student writers during the tough work of revising.

- Chapter 3, "Improving Texts: Advocating for Student Writing": An editor reads a text to give the writer substantive feedback. A multipurpose revision template (Four Reads) can help teacher–editors explore and bring new meanings to their texts.

- Chapter 4, "Connecting with Readers: Being Mindful of Purpose and Audience": Along with authors, editors bring new ideas and stories into the world of readers. This chapter delves into the importance of bringing greater awareness of the impact student texts can have on readers.

- Chapter 5, "Frequently Asked Questions About the Classroom Press": In this final chapter I review some questions that teachers often bring up when they consider taking up a teacher-as-editor model.

Roald Dahl benefited from the substantive feedback his editors provided. Because of editor suggestions, he deleted chapters and rewrote whole sections of his books. Our students deserve the same kind of attention and care. I want my students to know that as their editor, I've got their backs. As we become editors in our classroom publishing houses, we'll pass manuscripts back and forth as we work with students to publish texts that are the best they can be. Our classroom presses may be small, but together with our students, we can publish creative texts that explore big ideas.

I used to be a teacher
But now I'm a kid

I used to be sad
But now I'm a clown

I used to be stubborn
But now I'm a cheerleader

I used to be a little girl
But now I'm in third grade

Back *and* Forth

Introducing a Small Press Publishing Model to Student Writers

1

The classroom had that great buzz that's typical of writing workshop. There were a few idlers, but nearly everyone was writing, conferring, or illustrating. I was relieved to see that Becca had finished her draft and was placing it in the publishing box. When I read it over later that day, I could see that she had corrected some spelling and punctuation errors, but had done no revising. I jotted down some comments on sticky notes to prepare for our conference. Becca's story was fairly typical fifth-grade fare. A girl finds a rocket ship, travels to the moon, meets an alien, and suddenly wakes up in her own bed. In the end it turns out the main character was dreaming the entire time.

In my notes to Becca, I wrote, "Did the characters talk to each other? I'm curious about what they would say. Maybe add some dialogue?" Hoping for more descriptive details, I wrote two more questions: "What does the moon look like?" and "How does the character feel when she wakes up?"

The next day at our conference, Becca listened to my comments and answered my questions. When I asked her how she planned to revise, she told me, "I don't want to change it. I like it the way it is." I reminded her that authors revise their stories, and I hoped she would think about adding at least one more detail. As I began

working with another writer, I noticed Becca writing for a moment and then returning her draft back to the publishing box.

Becca had done exactly as I requested. She revised her story by adding a sentence about the moon's "GIGANTIC CRATERS!" I wasn't thrilled with her revision efforts, but I was pleased that she had actually finished a piece of writing. Becca had a history of starting stories, losing interest, and dropping them long before they were done. With this alien story, she had finished a draft, had conferred with peers and with me, and had done a bit of revising and proofreading. Though I thought her text was fairly bare bones, I felt that the story might be a turning point for Becca as a writer. I planned to send Becca off to the publishing center with her draft the next day.

At that time, we were lucky to have volunteers staffing our school publishing center a few mornings each week. After students took their stories through the writing process in the classroom, volunteers typed and bound them into books. Then students added illustrations.

I was surprised to see a publishing center volunteer at the classroom door later that day when the class was out at recess. She seemed uncomfortable. She held up Becca's story and said, "Do you really think this should be published? There's really not much to it. It's probably going to take me longer to type and bind this than it took Becca to write. "

I was taken aback by her comments and honestly, a little annoyed. I knew the story wasn't going to be nominated for a Caldecott Medal any time soon, but why shouldn't Becca get to publish it? Other students had certainly brought simpler stories to the publishing center and their drafts had been published without further revisions. I believed that publishing this first story could lead Becca toward better writing in the future. Maybe her next draft would be more detailed. I was trying to teach the writer, not the writing. Like other writing process teachers, I believed that Becca was in charge of her writing—not me and not the publishing center volunteers.

I told the volunteer that I would look over the story again with Becca and thanked her—through gritted teeth—for sharing her concerns with me. All day I could not get the conversation out of my mind. Gradually, I became less annoyed, but more and more embarrassed by the encounter. Why had I sent Becca to the publishing center with a draft that I believed wasn't high quality? I had put both of us in a bad situation. Becca's story had been critiqued harshly by one of her first readers, and my reputation as a writing teacher was potentially at risk as well. I wanted both of us to be proud of the writing in our room. How could I help Becca improve her story when she was happy with it in its present state? I wasn't sure how to proceed. I believed Becca was capable of more in her writing, but I didn't know how to help her improve without being pushy or overpowering about revisions.

Writing Research: Rethinking the Teacher's Role in Revision

As a process writing teacher, I presented myself as a fellow writer when I worked with Becca and her classmates. I shared my own writing with students and kept a notebook. I emphasized to students that they were in charge of their writing. I believed that my identity as a writer would transfer to my students as we shared our writing processes and products in writing workshop.

When I prepared for conferences, I always wrote on sticky notes, and when I met with students, I made sure that I kept my hands off their texts. When we conferred, I tried to take a light approach—asking questions, rather than offering specific suggestions. I agreed with Donald Graves' advice to only be directive with students when they can answer our conference questions with information that will support their writing (1994, 98). Regie Routman suggests that teachers use their own writing as instructional texts, and tells us if "we want students to take revision seriously and do it well, we will need to show them how, beginning with our own writing" (2000, 307). I had shown students many examples of how I had revised my texts. I had revised my drafts in front of the class during minilessons, but I wasn't seeing students revising their own drafts in ways that brought much change to their texts.

It took years, but I eventually began to accept that I was not helping students revise their writing. The modeling I was doing with my own writing didn't transfer to their work. When I didn't see students improving in their ability to revise, I just tried harder to be a fellow writer, a better supporter, a more active listener. I was probably taking the "fellow writer" approach a bit too seriously. Being a fellow writer in the classroom did not help students develop their own writing identities. Becca's lack of interest in revision was not atypical, and it was rare that students published stories that were radically different from their rough drafts.

Writing researcher Barbara Kamler believes that writing workshop conferences with students typically reveal a problematic "reluctance by teachers to interfere with the writer's personal voice" (2001, 63). Timothy Lensmire deals with similar concerns about teachers' roles in writing workshop in his book, *Powerful Writing, Responsible Teaching*. When teachers worry too much about honoring student control of texts, we may not be giving students the writing support they need. Lensmire considers teacher hesitation to get involved with students as they write as a kind of "abandonment":

> *It seems that children's freedom in the workshop is to be achieved more by leaving them alone than by engaging them in dialogue with others. In the name of not interfering in children's meaning-making, we may abandon them to it—free to express whatever they already are, but not helped to escape it.* (2000, 50)

In some ways I had abandoned Becca when I sent her to share a subpar text with the publishing center volunteer. Like the third-grade students Lensmire describes, student writers in my classroom were free to express their ideas in their stories, but weren't getting much help considering *new ideas*. Lensmire encourages writing teachers to enter into greater dialogue with students about their writing, taking up multiple viewpoints and story lines as they develop the ideas in their drafts (37).

Presenting myself as a fellow writer in the workshop helped my students see that I valued writing, but my strict interpretation of this role had prevented us from having productive conversations when it came to revising. Writing researchers like Kamler and Lensmire were focusing on these issues, but I wasn't finding much in the way of specific guidance when it came to how teachers could get more involved with writers during revision and I was still worried about overpowering students with my agenda.

Learning from Editors: Balancing Three Publishing Responsibilities

Reading more about the work professional editors do with published authors helped me change my approach to teaching writing. We all have read authors thanking their editors in acknowledgment sections. Many authors credit editors for helping them revise and improve their texts in other forums as well. On her website, Patricia Polacco (n.d.) tells readers that when she is done with a draft, she turns it over to her editor who then "asks me to write and rewrite many times until the story is perfect." It's interesting to contrast Polacco's editor's request to "write and rewrite many times" with my request to Becca that she make "at least one" revision to her alien story. Young adult author John Green discusses "the truth about book editors," on an episode of the Vlogbrothers vlog:

> Without Julie [Strauss Gabel] and before her my amazing mentor and first editor Eileen Cooper nothing anyone likes about Looking for Alaska would be in that book. In short . . . I'd like to think that writers are more important than editors. The truth is that we might not be. There's a reason that The Great Gatsby and The Sun Also Rises were edited by the same guy!

As a teacher it's hard to imagine giving the type of feedback to students that John Bellairs got from his editor. When the author of *The House with a Clock in Its Walls* sent his manuscript to Dial Books, an assistant editor told him that she would consider looking at his manuscript again if he would be willing to "cut it in half and make the main character the boy instead of the middle-aged uncle" (Fogelman 1993, 312). Instead of writing back, "No thanks! It's perfect right now," Bellairs chose to try out the editor's suggestions. One year later he resubmitted the revised manu-script. Bellairs' book was accepted and published and won a best book award from the *New York Times* in 1993. Author Christopher Paul Curtis likens the editor–writer relationship to the relationship between a student and a language arts teacher. Just as a "wise student" listens to a teacher's sugges-tions, Curtis feels an obligation to give serious consideration to his editor's feedback. Though Curtis doesn't take all of his editor's advice, he is open to her suggestions because he trusts that he and his editor share similar goals.

The back-and-forth of revising is crucial to the publishing process in real life. Where I held back with writers, fearing that I would take over control of projects, most editors take a "strong-minded" approach. Editor Robert Gottleib asks, "If you don't know what you think, or if you're nervous about expressing your opinion, what good is that to a writer?" (Lerner 2000, 218–19).

Editors are committed to getting writers to revise their texts, but how do they keep from overwhelming their writers with their suggestions? How do they bal-ance their goal of substantive revision with respect for the author's intentions and purposes? For editors, I learned that there is no set procedure to follow with every writer, but many editors feel that three general commitments guide their work. Editors pay close attention to relationship, to text, and to readership while assisting writers to revise.

Fostering Relationships

When editors and writers enter into the working relationship around a project, all have a specific role to play. Acknowledging that they wield more power in the relationship, editors take steps to make the relationship positive and productive. Editors make suggestions or point out problems, but ideally, writers come up with creative solutions in their revisions. In the publishing world, no one benefits if a writing relationship turns sour and the work doesn't lead to a publication. I now try to think of myself as a kind of publication partner while I work with writers, keeping the following questions in mind:

- How can I make the revision process part of a working relationship with student writers?

- How can I strive to keep the working relationship positive and productive?

- Are my suggestions leading to creative revisions by the writer?

Improving Texts

Editors view submitted drafts as changeable. They commit to revising texts extensively because texts represent high stakes for publishing houses. Texts that aren't high quality don't get published. In the past, I usually conferred with students once, maybe twice, before they published, but editors trade the work back and forth with writers as many times as needed. Now I make sure to do the same. Some students may need two to three conferences and some need more. I don't want students to publish something that lacks quality, so I make many suggestions. I consider the following questions as I work with texts published in my classroom:

- What potential meanings does this text hold?

- How can this text be revised to make it the best it can be?

Connecting with Readers

In the past, I worked with writers to make sure their drafts made sense but didn't discuss how their texts might impact future readers. Editors read manuscripts with special focus on potential readership. They analyze the purpose of a text, thinking of who will read it. They consider how readership can be increased. Now I discuss with students ways to connect with potential readers and how to increase interest in their texts. I keep in mind the following questions when thinking about my students' readers:

- How can I help the writer get ideas across to readers?

- How can this text bring new or original ideas to future readers?

These three commitments—to relationships, texts, and readers—make my role in the writing workshop more like an editor for my students. Although I still present myself as a fellow writer and make sure students know that writing is an important part of my life, I now switch gears when students are ready to revise. My students deserve more from me when they are working to publish. Before I offer my services as their editor, however, I introduce students to several important aspects of publishing.

Teacher as Editor: Getting Started with the Classroom Press

Most students don't have any idea about what's involved in publishing a book in the real world, and that may be a contributing factor to student resistance to revision. Few people know much about the way authors and editors work together. We may have heard about Max Perkins who worked with Hemingway and Fitzgerald, but not many other editors are household names. Although most students understand that publishing involves making a rough draft into a final draft or book, they don't know much beyond that. As they learn more about the work of authors and editors, their interest in revision naturally increases.

After writing and reading together during the first weeks of school, I tell students that it's time to start thinking about our classroom publishing house. Here are two introductory publishing activities followed by practical ways to transform your writing workshop to a small press.

Publishing Basics 101

Begin by asking students what they already know about publishing. A typical response might be that publishing involves "making a book." To show that there are many steps and stages involved in the publishing process, share several resources. Here are some introductory activities you might try:

- Look at Barbara Elleman's biography of Tomie dePaola (1999). Elleman shares a series of drafts from one of dePaola's picture books. It shows the different stages of a manuscript, from handwritten first draft to published book.

- Aliki's picture book *How a Book Is Made* (1988) gives younger students a good idea of the many different people who work in a publishing house. There are different types of editors. Explain that a lead (or developmental) editor works with authors to *shape and revise the ideas* in their books. A line (or copy) editor helps with grammatical issues, word choices, verb tense, and overall sense. Additionally, they assist with stylistic issues. Proofreaders help to correct misspellings, grammatical errors, typos, and the like that show up in proofs of the typeset pages. The publisher (HarperCollins 2017) has an online sampler of this book that makes it easy to share with a multimedia presenter.

- For older students, share the video series *How a Book Is Made* (www .wheredobookscomefrom.com/). Lauren Oliver (2012), author of *The Spindlers*, shares how her books go from manuscript to final publication at HarperCollins.

- *The School Story* (2001) by Andrew Clements is a great read-aloud for introducing publishing to students. This chapter book for middle grade readers follows a sixth-grade writer as she tries to get her book published.

During these activities, introduce the word *manuscript* as the term for a piece of writing before it is published. When talking about student drafts, use the term *manuscript* and students will quickly follow suit.

Publishing Scavenger Hunt

After learning some publishing fundamentals, students can go on a scavenger hunt. All books have publishers. You might hold up a book you've read together, saying, "We know the title and author of this book, but do we know who published it?" Locate the publisher on the binding of the book, and on the title page, and then fill out the first row on the scavenger hunt worksheet together (see Figure 1.1). Students can continue to locate publishing information from other books in the classroom to complete the worksheet (see Figures 1.2a–b).

Students enjoy this exploration activity and begin to see patterns in their findings. Certain publishers appear multiple times on their lists. This is a good introduction to learning more about the difference between large and small publishing houses.

Throughout the school year, share names of publishing companies whenever introducing a read-aloud. Students can identify publishers in their book talks and reviews as well throughout the school year.

Developing the Identity of the Classroom Press

Using a PowerPoint slide show, I share information about various publishing houses with students. A chart would be equally effective. I review brief historical information about the printing press. Before the printing press, books were scarce and had to be copied by hand, making literacy a rarity. The invention of printing presses led to more books being produced and more people reading. An avid reader once reacted to this information with an emphatic, "If I traveled back in time, I definitely would *not* want to travel before the printing press was invented." Students learn that the terms *publishing house* and *press* can be used interchangeably (see Figure 1.3).

Use web pages as mentor texts

Share two or three of your favorite publishers' web pages, pointing out the names, logos, and mission statements on each page. Explain to students that no matter the size of the press, all publishers have specific goals for their books. Even large presses that publish a variety of titles want submitted manuscripts that are well written and creative, with new ideas. No matter what the specific goal of the press, all presses start with writers who have ideas. Your students are the writers in your classroom

Name _____

Date _____ # _____

Publisher Scavenger Hunt

Title	Author	Publisher	Publisher Logo	Are you interested in reading this book? Rate your interest 1–5.

Figure 1.1 Publishing Scavenger Hunt Worksheet

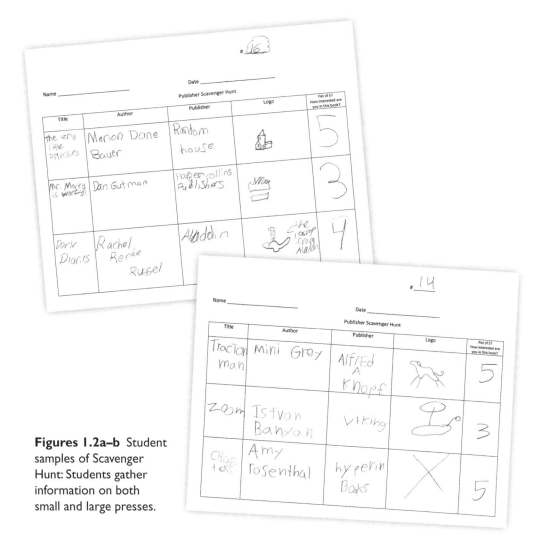

Figures 1.2a–b Student samples of Scavenger Hunt: Students gather information on both small and large presses.

Figure 1.3 Early Printing Press

press. When a book is accepted, editors work with writers to make their books the best they can be.

Introduce them to their editor

Students laugh when I introduce them to the editor (see Figure 1.4).

You may hear shouts of "You're our editor?" Confirm that you will indeed be their editor and that they'll be learning more about how editors and writers work together.

And they also have

. . . An EDITOR who works with authors to make their books the best they can be.

P.S.: That's going to be me!

Figure 1.4 Introduce yourself to students as an editor.

Develop criteria

In my classroom, I explain to the kids that we are going to publish books that are creative and well written, with surprising meanings, books that lead readers to have great discussions about important themes like friendship and fairness. You can develop your criteria for your classroom press based on elements of writing that are important to you as a teacher and to your school's literacy program. Read-aloud texts are great mentor texts to introduce the idea of *the list* of the classroom press. Publishing houses become known by the list of books that they publish. Every teacher has favorite texts they share with students. The published books we read aloud in our classrooms are excellent examples of original, cutting-edge writing that gets readers talking and thinking about new ideas. Using read-aloud texts as mentor texts in the writing workshop is standard operating procedure for most classroom teachers, but when introducing a classroom press model, these titles can also provide general guidelines as you develop criteria or goals for student publishing (see Figure 1.5).

Our press will be small, but we'll publish GREAT books!

We're looking for books that are:

Well written!

Original!

Surprising!

Powerful!

Figure 1.5 Share the goals of the classroom press.

After sharing the goals for the classroom press, ask students to help design a name and a logo for your press (see Figures 1.6 and 1.7). The logo should be eye-catching, easy to draw, and representative of the classroom in some way.

Some students may want to make two logos, one for the classroom press and one for their DIY publications. This is an exciting indication that students understand that there can be different ways to publish.

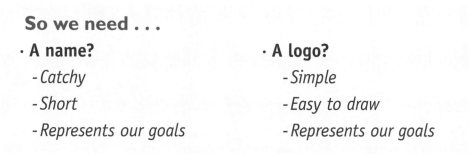

So we need . . .

· A name?	· A logo?
- Catchy	- Simple
- Short	- Easy to draw
- Represents our goals	- Represents our goals

Figure 1.6 Involve students in the creation of the classroom press.

Figures 1.7a–b Students design logos for their self-published DIY books.

You may want to keep the name of the press from year to year, but it's still fun to get students involved with the process of creating the classroom press. Once your class chooses the logo and name, make a simple web page or poster for the classroom to advertise your press (see Figure 1.8). A web page gives the press an official feeling

Popcorn Press in Room 200

- We are an independent classroom press.
- We publish original picture books that focus on social issues and important themes.
- At Popcorn Press, we publish books that POP!

Figure 1.8 Make the classroom press official with a simple web page, bulletin board, or classroom blog.

that students enjoy, but posters, flyers, or publishing bulletin boards can also work to announce that the classroom press is born! Popcorn Press is the name of our press, but each year students redesign its logo.

Publishing companies, especially smaller independent presses, are often associated with specific kinds of titles. It's important for authors to submit work that is in line with *the list* of the press to increase their chances of having their work considered.

To learn more about the list of a press, explore the "About Us" section on its web page. For example, visit Lee and Low's web page (www.leeandlow.com) for information about what they publish (see Figure 1.9). As you read over the guidelines for authors, take notes on chart paper, the board, or a digital tool. Students get the idea that some publishers are looking for specific kinds of manuscripts.

Students want to know about *unsolicited manuscripts.* Some presses don't want new authors to submit manuscripts. A large

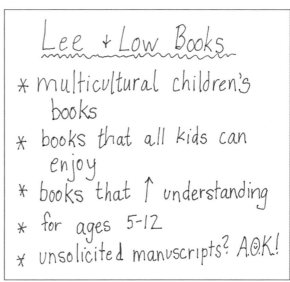

Figure 1.9 With your students, learn more about your favorite presses.

publisher's site like Scholastic will state that they do not accept unsolicited manuscripts. Large companies tend to work with authors who have already published with them, or with authors they seek out. This information shows students a key benefit of small press publishing. When I've asked, "Do we take unsolicited manuscripts at our press?" there are often mixed responses. Students aren't sure. I explain that we don't take unsolicited manuscripts, but that our press is soliciting, or asking, all of them, to publish their writing. Invariably someone asks something along the lines of, "If my little brother wants to publish with us, is that OK?" I usually couch my response by saying something like, "We may open up to other writers in the future. Let's see." Read three or four "About Us" statements on various web pages, and then begin to develop your own "About Us" section for your press.

Writing Proposals

Writers submit proposals with their manuscripts, where they share with the press some information about their manuscript. To get students comfortable with the idea of a proposal, we first fill out a proposal together in the role of one of our read-aloud authors. Figure 1.10 shows a mock proposal for *Voices in the Park*, by Anthony Browne (1998).

After students have practiced with proposal writing as a whole-class activity, they can begin submitting proposals with their own manuscripts (Figure 1.11). When you meet with students, start to point out that you may notice new meanings in their pieces that they may not have identified.

The proposal form gives some basic information about their pieces. It helps students distinguish between writing that's just for fun and writing for an audience.

Aug. 21

PUBLISHING PROPOSAL

Dear Popcorn Press,

Here's my manuscript! Please read it over and let me know what you think.

My title is _Voices in the Park_

I wrote about _kids going to the pand and meeting each other_

My theme is _Friendship and missunderstanding_

This theme is important to me because _I beleve people should get along_

I think my readers will like this writing because _It has great iullactations_

Would you please help me publish my excellent manuscript! I'm ready to revise the best book it can be!

Sincerely,

Anthromey Brown, Author!

Figure 1.10 Fill out mock proposals with a read-aloud text.

PUBLISHING PROPOSAL

Dear Popcorn Press,

Here's my manuscript! Please read it over and let me know what you think.

My title is _My Messy room_

I wrote about _my room and how it is always messy._

My theme is _about kids and adults having different opinions._

This theme is important to me because _I don't like cleaning my room._

I think my readers will like this writing because _It tells them something and its also funny._

Would you please help me publish my excellent manuscript! I'm ready to revise with an editor to make it the best book it can be!

Sincerely,

_____, Author!

Figure 1.11 Publishing proposals help kids gain awareness about what writers do in real-world publishing.

Simulating Editor and Author Conversations

At this point, students should know some basics of publishing. They understand that publishing involves both effort and patience. I like to tell students about the writer James Lee Burke. Burke has published dozens of books, but his first novel was rejected one hundred and eleven times. He worked at other jobs for nine years before a publisher finally accepted his manuscript. We discuss the possible reasons why James Lee Burke kept submitting his manuscript to dozens of publishers. He believed writers should never be discouraged by rejection and under no circumstances give up on submitting work (Burke 2015). Receiving a book contract is usually the beginning of more hard work, but the author is assisted in this work by the services of a professional editor.

Students are surprised to learn how much revision authors do, even after they are established writers. Share information from Patricia Polacco's website about how her editor makes suggestions for rewriting. You might also share Kate DiCamillo's examples of how her stories grow from manuscript to publication (Scholastic n.d.).

It's interesting to point out that even after four drafts, DiCamillo changes her draft again based on suggestions made by her editor. As students take notes, share examples of the different suggestions editors might make. I share images of manuscripts that have gone through many revisions. Barry Cunningham, J. K. Rowling's editor, suggested that Rowling remove an entire scene out of the second Harry Potter book (*The Telegraph* 2010). I ask students how that must have felt to the author and why she would agree to do it.

When editors read a manuscript, they make comments about parts of the manuscript that are good and parts that can be made better. Editors ask questions and make suggestions for changes. They might even give suggestions for new topics for authors to write about. Holding up the books of various authors, I share stories with students about their work with editors.

Tomie dePaola has worked with his editor for over thirty years. His editor even has a page on his website. Even though

they've worked together for so many years, they don't always agree on revisions and they argue about some decisions.

Ursula Nordstrom is an editor of many books students know and love. Hold up books by Maurice Sendak and E. B. White and Shel Silverstein. Examples of Nordstrom's back-and-forth correspondence with these editors appear in a collection called *Dear Genius*, edited by Leonard Marcus (1998). You can share pictures of Nordstrom from the web so that students know she was a real person, who had strong, long-standing relationships with some of their favorite authors.

Over the course of decades, Nordstrom gave many suggestions to writers. She was even the person that suggested to Shel Silverstein that he write poetry for kids.

An editor and author work together to make sure a book is the best it can be. Even though the work may take a long time, sometimes years, editors and writers trade the manuscript back and forth many times, working through changes. Students learn that editors and writers aren't usually in the same place, so the work is mostly done through phone calls, letters, and emails.

Have students pair up to write short dialogues between an author and an editor. Their dialogues should contain references to information they've learned in the editor minilesson. Students can present their dialogues to the class. These are usually quite amusing, but also provide playful demonstrations that revision work can involve negotiations and give-and-take (see Figure 1.12a–b).

After students present their skits, talk about the revision work. In their dialogues, students usually point out that publishing takes time and involves changes to books and that the editor makes all kinds of suggestions.

I ask the class, "Are you ready to start working with your editor at Popcorn Press?" There may be a few students who aren't sure about this work, but most are enthusiastic. One student responded, "Once I get a contract, I'll be ready. You should make contracts for us." These lessons get students comfortable with the process of revision that's so critical to the publishing process. Simulating a small press with students provides opportunities for playful, imaginative activities that students enjoy.

Author Toni Morrison writes that sometimes she finds passages that don't quite work as she reads books (Schappell 1993). A former editor herself, she wishes the

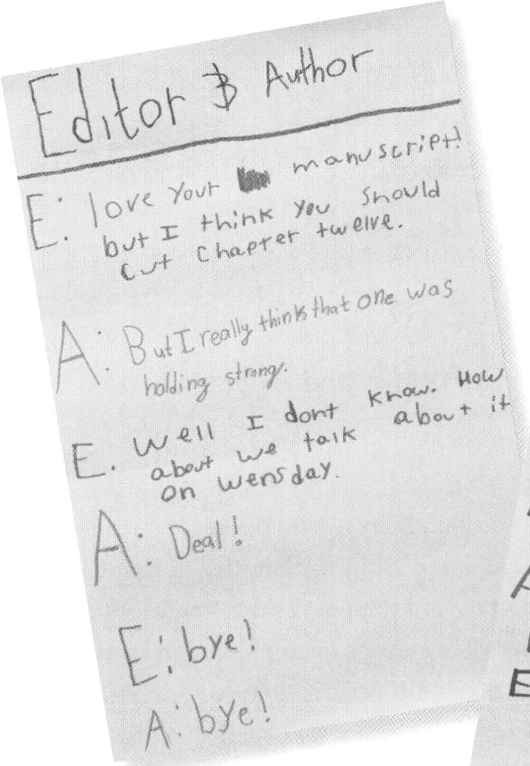

Editor ↓ Author

E: I love your ~~[scribble]~~ manuscript! but I think you should cut chapter twelve.

A: But I really think that one was holding strong.

E: Well I dont know. How about it about we talk on wensday.

A: Deal!

E: bye!

A: bye!

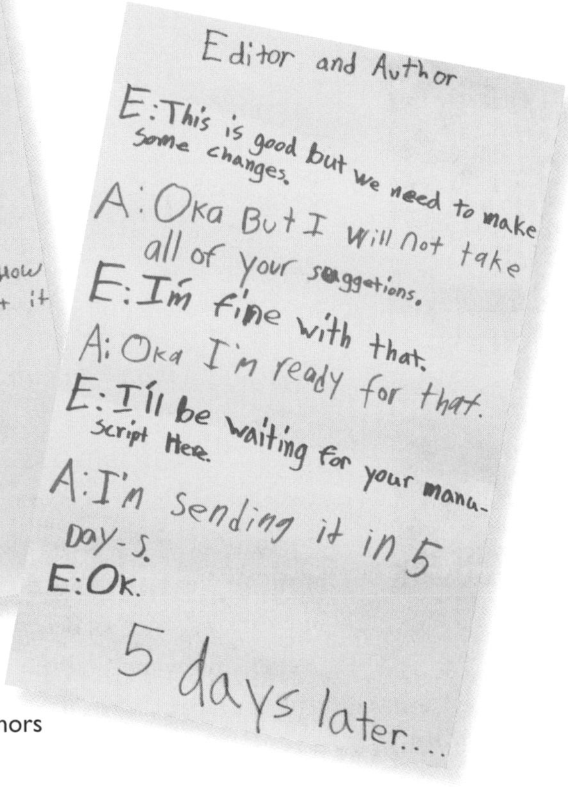

Editor and Author

E: This is good but we need to make some changes.

A: Oka But I will not take all of your suggestions.

E: I'm fine with that.

A: Oka I'm ready for that.

E: I'll be waiting for your manuscript Here.

A: I'm sending it in 5 Day-s.

E: Ok.

5 days later....

Figures 1.12a–b Playful Explorations of Student–Authors Working with Their Editors

author had worked with a more careful editor. I wish I had known about publication lists and writing proposals and editor–writer relationships in my early days of teaching writing workshop. Becca's story about a girl and an alien could have turned into something exciting had I acted as her editor. Together we could have focused on developing her story's theme. Guided by editors and their work with writers, I now see that Becca's story could have been revised to highlight ideas around home, friendship, or communication.

Now I know more about how to work with writers to revise their texts, even those who like their writing "just as it is." In the next chapter, I'll discuss ways that an editor builds a relationship of trust and camaraderie with writers to make the writing relationship both productive and positive.

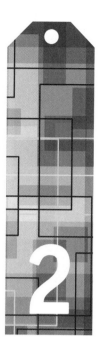

Fostering Relationships
Keeping Revision Work Positive and Productive

Nara was a high-achieving student who seemed naturally good at everything she did in school. English was her second language and she loved to write, taking pride in her lengthy, descriptive stories. Unlike Becca, Nara spent days on a draft and was known among her classmates as an "awesome writer." Though their writing identities were quite different, Nara responded to revision suggestions much as Becca did, frequently expressing confusion or even annoyance, telling me, "Nah, I don't want to change it."

Revision is difficult for most, if not all, writers, so Nara's reactions weren't surprising. Where Becca seemed to have little investment in the writing process, Nara was overly attached to her pieces. She was comfortable with her place among her peers as a superior writer. Writing was her thing and she saw revision suggestions as an affront to her established writing identity.

Nara's proficiency as a writer had given her a skewed vision of revision work. Like most students, she knew little of the working relationship between writers and editors. Many authors describe the job of revising as long, difficult, emotional work. As with any collaborative project, publishing involves tensions as well as satisfactions. As teachers, when we engage in any kind of group work with colleagues, we accept that there will be a give-and-take to the work. When we help our students develop this ability to give and take in their revision work, we help them acquire a real-world skill that they can use for the rest of their lives. When we enter into a revision relationship with our students, we bring more authenticity to the writing workshop and better prepare them for the demands of collaborative work (whether in or out of the publishing business) in the future.

Writing Research: Lightening Up About Text Ownership

Writing workshop researchers advise teachers to make listening a priority when conferring with students. Instead of offering suggestions, teachers "follow the child" (Lensmire 2000, 45). Lucy Calkins advises, "Our job in a writing conference is to put ourselves out of a job, to interact with students in such a way that they learn how to interact with their own developing drafts" (1994, 229). Although helping students develop as independent writers is important, our attempts to follow the child may result in missed opportunities to challenge our students to rethink and reimagine their ideas and stories (Lensmire 2000). Carl Anderson has written that students do benefit from "honest feedback" during writing conferences, especially when teachers give students, who are usually unprepared for intensive revision suggestions, a heads-up that we intend to share "critical feedback about their writing work" (2000, 59).

Teachers know the importance of building strong relationships with students. To build writing relationships, we may need to move from a "follow the child" approach to a more interactive style of conferring. Lad Tobin calls for us to:

> Move beyond either/or thinking—either we have authority or they do; either we own the text or they do; either the meaning is in the writer or in the reader. . . . Rather than dichotomizing the teacher's and the student's roles, we need to see how they are inseparably related. (1993, 20)

Teachers and students, like editors and authors, have dissimilar roles to play in the production of classroom texts. When we take up an editor's role, we are no longer fellow writers, there only for encouragement and support. Writing researchers like Tobin believe that teachers can respect the authority of the writer while negotiating significant revisions of student texts. We can look to the working relationships of editors with published authors as we become more interactive with our writing conferences.

Learning from Editors: Working Relationships with Authors

Each publishing project is unique and so, therefore, is each working relationship between editor and author, but in the challenging work of publishing, the balance of power in the relationship generally tilts toward the editor. Author Jane Yolen cautions fellow writers, "Know this about being published: it is out of your hands. Even if you do everything you can think of to affect that outcome you cannot *make* an editor take your work" (2003, 17). When an editor does accept a writer's work, the two parties enter into a working relationship. Editor Maron Waxman asserts, "It is the editor's job to maintain a good working relationship with the author" (1993, 161). The adage that with power comes responsibility is particularly appropriate when it comes to publishing projects. Editors and writers both must compromise and negotiate while working together, but the editor, who holds a significant amount of power, must take on greater responsibility for making the relationship work.

When editors and writers work together, they trade texts back and forth, negotiating revisions on the path to publication. Gross describes the publishing house as a "senate" where the editor "should 'advise,' but the author must always 'consent'" (1993, xvi). Although the balance of power is rarely equal, writers are never powerless in the revision relationship. An editor can be strategic about persuading the author to make changes she considers necessary, but an author can reject editorial suggestions. Though there are undoubtedly more situations where a writer feels

overpowered by an editor than the other way around, writers have the ultimate say about whether a revision becomes part of a book. They also can walk away from editors, miss deadlines, and even attempt to bully the publishing house with unreasonable demands. Annoyed with Roald Dahl's behavior, Robert Gottlieb wrote to him, "You have behaved to us in a way I can honestly say is unmatched in my experience for overbearingness and utter lack of civility" (Treglown 1994, 215). When he sent out the letter to Dahl, the editorial staff at Knopf stood and applauded. Even when the writer and the editor have productive, trusting relationships, revision work is emotional and involves strategizing, negotiations, and compromise.

Editorial suggestions ideally assist the writer and are phrased in such a way that the author trusts that the editor is helpful rather than oppressive. Author Charles McGrath felt that his editor, Robert Gottlieb, possessed "an uncanny knack for putting his finger on that one sentence, or that one paragraph, that somewhere in the back of your mind you knew wasn't quite right" (Lerner 2000, 202). When the relationship works, writer and editor understand one another and both parties benefit as an editor's comments lead to creative revisions.

Writers invest so much of themselves in the writing of a text, so they may not always react with enthusiasm to editorial suggestions. Suggesting revisions is tricky work, and editors recognize that being tactful with writers is the best way forward. Teachers know the importance of tact when it comes to our interactions with students. As we teach, we negotiate, coach, discuss, suggest. Given the wide range of strategies we use to help our students meet their learning goals each day, it's surprising that with writing we often choose to back off and stay silent. Perhaps we hesitate because we don't want to interfere with the creativity of our students.

Learning from editors how best to work with writers can help us during our writing conferences. Editors employ a range of tactics that we can adopt and adapt for use in our workshops.

Although not all editors use the same set of procedures with authors, there are general strategies that editors seem to use (from a review of articles by and about professional editors). These guidelines can help us in our classrooms as we work more like editors when publishing student writing.

- Editors and authors trade the text back and forth as often as necessary. Every text is different and one size does not fit all when it comes to revisions. There's no set process for publishing a text. Some texts require more revision and some less.

- Editors prioritize the changes they think should be made to texts. They know that they might not get all the changes they hope for in a text, so certain changes may be ranked as more essential than others.

- Editors aim to be tactful with their suggestions. Instead of demanding changes, they may pose suggestions as questions to the writer, asking, "Is this section necessary?" or "Dialogue needed here?" If an editor does end up rewriting a small section of the text to show the author possible revision directions, she points out these changes to the author, clearly leaving tracks in the text.

- Because editors consider themselves to be advocates for texts as well as for writers, they take pains to communicate clearly about why they consider certain revisions to be essential.

Editors are committed to getting writers to revise their texts in specific ways. Using both tact and tactics, Ursula Nordstrom employed a "dazzling variety of means, including flattery, exhortation, extravagant praise, outrageous wit, guilt, self-parody, and self-deprecation" (Marcus 1998, xxvii–xxix). Nordstrom used to write to her authors that her edits were only suggestions and that she assumed the writer would think of something better than the ideas she proposed. In a letter to author John Steptoe, she assured him that his intention for the text guided her suggestions and that it was her job to determine *when* the text accurately reflected his intentions

(245). Maurice Sendak worked with Nordstrom for decades. He trusted her so completely that he believed his manuscript was only finished "when my editor thinks it's finished" (1990, 60).

Teacher as Editor: A Bolder Approach to Revision Work

We enter into a satisfying working relationship with students when we adopt an editor stance in the writing workshop, but before we get started, we need to be transparent with students about this shift in our identity. Most adults in our culture know little about the working relationship between an author and an editor, so the ins and outs of the publication relationship will certainly be unclear to students. You may hear students ask questions like, "What if I don't want to revise?" or "Can I say no to your suggestions?" This reaction is natural, given students' lack of awareness of how authors benefit from their work with editors. Students will need clarity about what to expect as they begin revision work with you.

Students may not know how a *working relationship* is different from other kinds of relationships. A writing conference with classmates, where student writers give one another support and share ideas, may or may not result in revisions of their texts. When they submit a manuscript to their editor, however, their manuscript will be going through significant changes to get it ready to publish. In a positive working relationship, people focus on achieving specific goals and may perform different roles. This is the case with writers who work with editors. The publishing relationship has been compared to a kind of symbiosis (Gross 1993). With symbiosis, each partner has her own important job to do, and each partner benefits.

Exploring Symbiosis in Publishing Relationships

Share photographs of symbiotic relationships in nature to help students more clearly understand the idea of symbiosis. In many writing workshops, students have come to see the teacher as a fellow writer, so this idea may be unsettling for them at first. Using pictures, explain that when you work with student writers, you'll have a job and they'll have a different job, but together, you'll have the same goal—to publish the best book possible (Figure 2.1).

Figure 2.1 Point out the distinct benefits and roles of symbiotic relationships in nature, using pictures such as this one.

It surprises students to learn that many authors feel grateful for, rather than burdened by, the help they get from editors. It's easy to find tributes to editors in the acknowledgment sections of the books we read aloud to students. Often, authors claim that their book was much improved through the revision work with their editor. A favorite author of my students is Newbery Medal–winner Katherine Applegate, author of *The One and Only Ivan* (2013). Applegate describes herself as lucky to have worked so hard on revising her manuscripts with editor Anne Hoppe. In the excerpt from an interview shown in Figure 2.2, Applegate talks

Figure 2.2 This interview with author Katherine Applegate shows how interactive revision work can be (Bird 2013).

Symbiotic Relationships?	
Each partner has a job to do.	• Was Anne Hoppe always your editor at HarperCollins? • Yeah, and you know *Ivan* would not be *Ivan* without Anne. Honestly, it was the most collaborative and fun adventure I've ever had with an editor. I was working on another animal fantasy, actually, and struggling with it. Anne finally looked at me, and she said, "You know, you really want to write that gorilla book, don't you?" I said, "Yeah, I really do."
Each partner relies on the other.	• . . . So, I went back to my original idea, and it really fell into place. Anne loves words the same way I do, and so we could go back and forth for three days trying to get a sentence just right.
Each partner benefits from the partnership.	• I love that. She'd say, "No that's not quite right." "Ok, we'll try again." And when you have that experience with an editor, you just feel so lucky."

Source: www.slj.com/2013/03/interviews/the-one-and-only-how-katherine-applegate-created-a-classic-and-nabbed-the-newbery/

about working with Hoppe for three days to get one sentence "right." Upon hearing this, one student exclaimed, "That's a really long book, so that must have taken a long time if they spent so much time on one sentence!" Students are surprised to learn that revising isn't a one-shot deal. It takes time and effort, and the editor supports the writer in the quest to make the book the best it can be.

As you talk about the editor and author relationship, have students create a graphic organizer to show the roles authors and editors play in the working relationship (Figure 2.3). As you fill in the graphic organizer, begin with the shared purpose in the center of the map. In an ideal relationship, editors and authors trade the book back and forth. Although writers write the manuscript, editors read the text and think about how it can be improved. Editors suggest changes to make sure the text matches the intentions of the writer. Writers consider the editors' suggestions and revise the text creatively. Writers and editors communicate with each other about the changes. Sometimes there is negotiation, sometimes there is compromise, but the editor does not change a book without the writer's approval. In the end, the writer is the author of the text, and the editor is the publisher of the text.

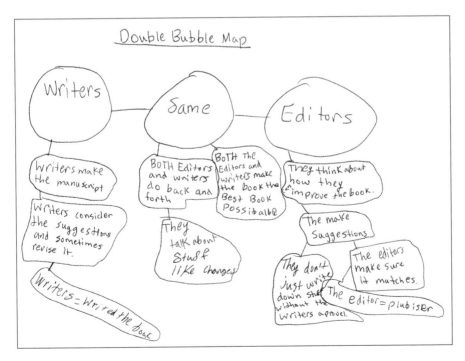

Figure 2.3
Double Bubble maps show the ways editors and writers are the same and the ways they are different.

When editor Ursula Nordstrom wrote to authors, she often began her letters with the greeting, "Dear Genius. . . ." It's important that our students know that we value and admire their creativity and their talent. Communicate to them that you are excited about working with them as their editor in the classroom publishing house. (See Figure 2.4.)

Getting to Know Student Attitudes About Revision

It's up to both editor and writer to make sure the working relationship is productive and rewarding. Have your students write a quick reflection about their revision histories. You will get a feel for how they perceive the revision work ahead. As students reflect on their revision histories, their attitudes and apprehensions about the upcoming project may emerge. Some students will be excited about this new relationship with their writing teacher and will be eager to delve into the publishing project (Figure 2.5).

Other students may reveal that they have not revised much in the past. They probably suspect, wisely, that revision work is not going to be easy. (See Figures 2.6 and 2.7.)

Figure 2.4 Students respond to a positive approach. Let them know that you're excited about the work you'll do together in your classroom press.

Dear Geniuses . . .

- I've shared with you some of the books I've edited in past years. I work hard to help writers at Popcorn Press publish great books that explore important themes.
- I'm looking forward to working with you to publish your writing. Every editing relationship is unique. Write me a note about our upcoming project.
- Have you done much revising with editors in the past? Can you tell me how that worked for you?
- What are your wishes for the picture book you are writing now? What do you want readers to TAKE AWAY from your book?
- Are you ready to get going?

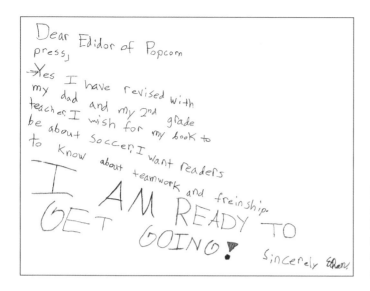

Figure 2.5 When students know about how editors and authors work together, they become excited and curious.

You may have students, like Nara, who are extremely attached to their first drafts. These students are naturally apprehensive about the prospect of trading their story back and forth with someone who expects their story to change.

Figure 2.6 and 2.7 It's common for students to express that they've done little revision in the past.

It's important to give students a heads up about what is involved with the back-and-forth revision work. When students learn that their favorite authors have trusting revision relationships with editors, they begin to accept the importance of revising, and they come to see suggestions made by their teachers as a form of support.

Preparing a Manuscript for Submission to the Classroom Press

A new focus on publishing does not change your writing workshop routines. Early in the school year, I teach lessons about the nuts-and-bolts of the writing process, just as I have in years past. Charts are displayed to help remind students about the stages their manuscripts will go through on the way to publication. Students know that publishing involves proofreading, revising, and conferring. Over the years, I've used a variety of forms to help students proofread and revise their drafts, independently and through peer conferences. My current revision template allows students to revise in three different ways, as well as proofread as they confer with peers. We call this format *Four Reads Revision* because students will read their draft four times to different classmates, each time focusing on a different aspect of the writing process. (See Figure 2.8.)

Because we've looked over the multiple drafts of favorite authors like Tomi de-Paola and Katherine Applegate, students know that authors revise their drafts many times before submitting them to a publishing house. The Four Reads Revision template lets students see themselves as authors, committed to sharing and improving their manuscripts. Although it is uncommon for most students to produce significant revisions on their own, using the template gets students reading over their drafts multiple times to different classmates. Some students make many changes and others make only a few. I introduce the template by filling it out with students, using one of our read-aloud texts so that students become comfortable with the form and can use it as a guide when having conferences with classmates. The template helps students focus on the important elements of writing and has four sections:

1. green read: focus on meanings

2. orange read: focus on craft

3. blue read: focus on themes and issues

4. red read: proofread for language conventions.

Green Read: Meaning Making	Orange Read: Writer's Craft	Blue Read: Critical Literacy
List 2 or 3 ideas readers might consider after reading your manuscript.	Revise in **ORANGE** to:	Revise in **BLUE** to:
Revise in **GREEN** to make your meanings stronger.	_____ Make your lead a HOOK!	_____ highlight a social issue or important theme that you believe readers need to know about and talk about.
	_____ Add 2 power words on each page.	
•	_____ Add one snapshot on each page.	
•	_____ Make sure your ending stays with us even after we are done reading.	
•		
gave me a green suggestion:	**gave me an orange suggestion:**	**gave me a blue suggestion:**

Red Read: Proofreading

I found and fixed _____ **CUPS** errors. (**C**apitals, **W**ord **U**sage, **P**unctuation, **S**pelling)

Figure 2.8 Four Reads Revision Template

Green Read

By second grade, we want students to compose pieces that go beyond the basic "bed-to-bed" piece, describing events with simple details about the beginning, middle, and end. Students can and should explore themes, concepts, and big ideas in their writing. The green read asks students to identify multiple meanings in their texts. Students write down two or three ideas that they believe will come through to readers. Using a green pencil, they try to revise their draft so that one of these ideas

Figure 2.9 Writers confer with classmates for different purposes.

is made stronger. Next, they read their draft to a classmate (Figure 2.9), share their meanings, and ask for a suggestion. It's OK if they don't get a suggestion from a peer. The meanings the students identify are helpful guides when we confer later.

Orange Read

We want students to be able to craft their narratives to enhance the reading experience for their audience. The orange read asks students to revise in orange to improve their leads, add power words and figurative language, and make sure their endings leave readers thinking.

Blue Read

With the blue read, students highlight a social issue or important theme in their text that they want readers to know and talk about. Even in very simple pieces, students should develop themes. Sample themes could be family, friendship, imagination, or nature. After identifying a theme for their piece, students try to add a blue revision that enhances the theme in some way (Figure 2.10). They also share their theme with a partner and then ask for a blue suggestion (Figure 2.11).

Red Read

Students proofread their drafts with the classic red pen. They try to find and fix any errors that have to do with CUPS—capitals, word usage, punctuation, and spelling. We proofread last, after we've focused on the important ideas and the craft elements of our manuscripts.

When the template is filled out and the manuscript has been revised to the best of the student's ability, students fill out a proposal form and submit their manuscript to the classroom press. It's not important that the revision template is filled out completely, nor is the color coding the most important thing. The template is valuable because it gets students in the habit of reading their draft over several times with their peers and getting specific kinds of feedback. The template also serves as a formative assessment tool in that it highlights where students are strong with revision and where they need extra support.

Figure 2.10 Students use different colors to make different kinds of changes to their texts.

Figure 2.11 Students discuss drafts with classmates.

Guidelines for Working Productively with Student–Authors

Because you've built up your students' background knowledge of ways editors work with authors, they will be expecting you to be more involved with their revision work. Many will be curious to see how their teacher's new role plays out during writing workshop. If you've exposed them to examples of how well-known authors produce multiple drafts while working with editors, they have seen that revision will take time and effort. They will also anticipate a new kind of support from their teacher–editor. This is exciting territory to enter into with your students. Not only does the work vary from student to student, it allows for unique and creative interactions with student–authors. Let's take a close look at one student's process. Figure 2.12 shows Nara's story over time. Figure 2.12a is an example of Nara's first page of her story as it began to change over multiple drafts. Nara wrote a story about a friendship that falls apart. She focused on the theme of exclusion. Her story resolves when the friends reunite years later, as adults. Notice the embedded typed suggestions in italics and her responses to my queries in pencil. Nara and I passed her story back and forth five times before it was published. Although revising took a lot of work, it was gratifying to Nara to see her story develop and change over the course of our work together.

Even though students have been given the heads-up that they will be doing more intensive revision than they have in the past, revision work will involve ups and downs, emotions and tensions. Some manuscripts will need many revisions; others will need less, and there is no rigid protocol or set process to follow. The path to publication can be a rocky one, but revisiting the general guidelines gleaned from editor literature can help to keep the work productive and positive. As you enter into revision relationships with student writers, it will be helpful to:

- prepare the text for the back-and-forth

- focus on high-priority revisions

- be tactful when making suggestions

- communicate clearly.

Prepare the text for the back-and-forth

To get ready for the back-and-forth of the publishing project, it is best to work with a typed draft, saved as a word-processing file. Many elementary students are surprisingly adept at word processing, but if you find this to be too time-consuming for some, you can type their drafts or have a volunteer do the typing for the press. Once a draft is saved as a word-processing file, you can add student revisions to the draft as you pass the draft back and forth over several writing sessions.

Over time, students will be excited to see concrete changes to their stories as they get closer and closer to publication.

As you read through student drafts, type your suggestions directly into the draft. Follow your suggestions by inserting a few inches of blank space, so students can respond right on the paper copy. Distinguish your suggestions from student text by

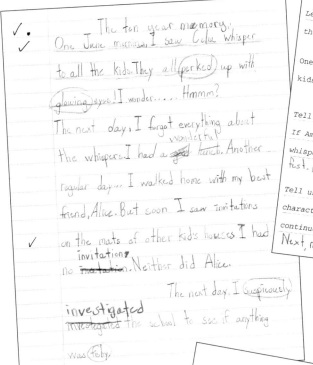

Figure 2.12a Nara fixed spelling errors with a red marker and circled powerful words.

The ten year memory,
One June morning, I saw Celia whisper
to all the kids. They all (perked) up with
(glowing eyes.) I wonder..... Hmmm?
The next day, I forgot everything about
the whispers. I had a ~~good~~ wonderful hunch. Another
regular day... I walked home with my best
friend, Alice. But soon I saw invitations
✓ on the mats of other kid's houses I had
no ~~invitation~~ invitations. Neither did Alice.
                The next day, I (suspiciously)
investigated ~~investagated~~ the school to see if anything
was (fishy)

Figure 2.12b When Nara receives her typed draft, she responds to her editor's suggestions with revisions. Editor's suggestions are embedded in the text in italics (they are underlined as well).

The Ten Year Memory
*Lead: What should we see? Set up the scene. Is
the main character walking into the school?*
One ~~June~~ April morning, Happy as a clam, ready to start my day. I turned a corner and I saw Celia whisper to all the
kids. They all perked up with glowing eyes!
I wondered....Hmmmm? Did she get a new friend?
*Tell a bit more here…
If Amarilla was friends with Celia, why is Celia
whispering about her?* She isn't. She's talking about the
rest. Celia is betraying Amarilla.
*Tell us how the rest of the day went? Did the
character forget about the incident? Or did she
continue to think about it?* She continued to think.
Next, next day tells.

Figure 2.12c With her next draft, Nara can see the story taking shape. She continues to revise, responding to suggestions embedded in her text.

The Ten Year Memory
One April morning, happy as a clam, I walked
into school, ready to start my day. When I turned
a corner, I saw Celia whispering to all the kids.
They all perked up with glowing eyes!
I wondered...Hmmmm? Did she get a new friend? I was about
to walk up but I tried to forget about it.
*Tell a bit more here. Why didn't Amarilla walk up?
Was there something in Celia's face that made her
not want to approach?*
I continued to think about Celia for the rest
of the day. What was she thinking? My mind was a scrapbag
picking ideas out. Finally the bell rang. I went home alone
Tell us how the rest of the day went? Give us a wondering.
I seemed Celia was spending more and more time with
few more details about this? Does she see Celia the 8th
again that day? graders than
with me.

continues

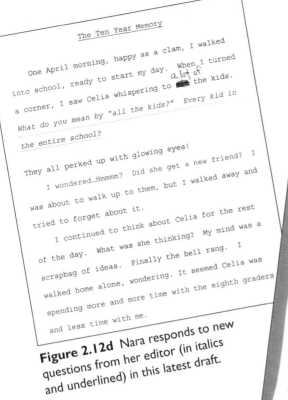

The Ten Year Memory

One April morning, happy as a clam, I walked into school, ready to start my day. When I turned a corner, I saw Celia whispering to *a lot of* the kids. *What do you mean by "all the kids?"* Every kid in the entire school?

They all perked up with glowing eyes!

I wondered...Hmmmm? Did she get a new friend? I was about to walk up to them, but I walked away and tried to forget about it.

I continued to think about Celia for the rest of the day. What was she thinking? My mind was a scrapbag of ideas. Finally the bell rang. I walked home alone, wondering. It seemed Celia was spending more and more time with the eighth graders and less time with me.

Figure 2.12d Nara responds to new questions from her editor (in italics and underlined) in this latest draft.

The Ten Year Memory

One April morning, happy as a clam, I walked into school, ready to start my day. When I turned a corner, I saw Celia whispering to a lot of eighth grade kids. They all perked up as they listened with glowing eyes!

I wondered...Hmmmm? Did Celia get a new friend? I was about to walk up to them, but I walked away and tried to forget about it.

I continued to think about Celia for the rest of the day. What was she thinking? My mind was a scrapbag of ideas. Finally the bell rang. I walked home alone, wondering. We had been best friends for years. We were both in the seventh grade. We both had the same hobbies like reading and writing. It seemed Celia was now spending more and more time with her new eighth grade friends and less time with me. I couldn't understand why.

The next day, I forgot everything about the whispers. I asked Celia if she could eat with me. She said, "Sure." We sat at a table. I was having a wonderful lunch with Celia when I noticed she seemed to be winking at the other girls. What was going on?

Figure 2.12e Nara's story is ready for illustrations and binding.

using italics or bold font. A student volunteer can help you introduce the format to the class. I usually ask an enthusiastic writer to volunteer for this demonstration at first. I give the student a heads-up about the format of the demonstration and make sure that she wants to participate. While the student holds a paper copy of her draft as well as a pencil, the story is projected on to a screen so the class can see how the suggestions are embedded in the text. Have a conversation with the student–author about your suggestions. Talk through possible ideas for revisions. Students get excited about this demonstration and many ask if their stories can be used for revision demonstration minilessons as well.

Focus on high-priority revisions

As you first read student drafts, you're going to catch problems and issues that the writer did not catch. It's not unusual for first drafts to be confusing, repetitive, or bare bones. Often students veer off into tangents that either do not move their texts along or fail to develop their themes. As you read, ask yourself questions about the three main revision domains:

- **Meaning:** Do all parts of this story make sense? Are any sections unnecessary or repetitive?

- **Craft:** Does the lead hook the reader? Does the ending leave the reader thinking? Could the author add any descriptive details?

- **Theme:** Is the author's theme coming across? Did the author pursue a theme or social issue that can be explored in more depth?

As you add suggestions to the draft, you may feel that some changes are essential, others less so. Though it may feel awkward or overly pushy to be embedding suggestions throughout the draft, remember that you are helping your students by pointing out issues that may distract their readers or, even worse, could cause readers to turn away from their stories, due to confusion or boredom. In your first read through, you may want to only insert suggestions that you believe must result in revision for the text not only to make sense but to clarify the author's intent. Nara chose the theme of exclusion for a manuscript about a girl who does not get invited to a party. When she veered off course from this central theme, I could point out where she needed to revise to get this theme to come across to her writers. I could also point out sections that could be deleted because they distracted the reader with irrelevant or repetitive information.

Accept that you might not get everything you ask for. Top-priority suggestions can be the focus of initial writing conferences. For example, Allen wrote a story about a character who can't get friends to play outside because they want to stay inside and play video games. At the end, the main character's mom called all the other moms to discuss the problem. The next day the moms made the kids play outside. I thought Allen's ending was problematic; not only is the main character unable to resolve his own conflicts, Allen relied on an ending that showed no character development or struggle. I knew a new ending

would be a high-priority revision. At our conference, Allen was intrigued when I suggested that the character should do something clever to solve his own problems rather than rely on his mother. Allen and I discussed possible endings. A new ending was a significant revision, but I felt it to be essential to Allen's story. In later conferences, we addressed other issues such as creating realistic dialogue and making sure all scenes connect back to his plotline. As an experienced reader, you'll know how to prioritize your suggestions. Focus on issues that disrupt the reader's enjoyment, experience, and understanding of the text.

Be tactful when making suggestions

Editors know to be tactful when making suggestions about manuscripts. They often phrase their suggestions as queries rather than demands. You can see some of the ways I attempted to make suggestions in a tactful, courteous way to Nara in her drafts. A respectful, lighthearted tone is always our aim as teachers when we interact with students. With writing, it's especially important. When pointing out problems with student texts, questions help to get the writers thinking about possibilities. When you ask questions in the draft, it's helpful to pair your question with a suggestion. This shows the author that you are there to support their work, not just to point out issues.

- "Would kids really talk like this? Maybe they would say . . ."

- "Where are your characters at this point? What should we see and hear?"

- "This might be a good spot for some dialogue. What did the characters say when they found out about this problem?"

When working with Nara's text, I tried to phrase my suggestions clearly, but respectfully. I tried to make suggestions when I felt the text was confusing or needed more specific details. When a scene change was unclear, I asked, "Where is Celia at this point? What should the reader see?" If I didn't phrase a suggestion as a question, I tried to express the idea in an open-ended way, writing, "Maybe you want the characters to meet for lunch at this point?"

When students read your questions, they start thinking of responses. When you meet, your questions are all laid out in the text and students will have had some time to consider changes. This time lag helps take some of the immediate emotion out of revision work because students have time to read over your questions and consider them before you meet face-to-face.

If you have questions about a student's text, future readers are probably also going to have those questions. Although you certainly don't want to bombard students with too many questions, keep in mind that you are helping writers to identify and resolve problems within their texts, shielding them from future criticism once their work is published. You don't want your students' readers to be confused or to lose interest as they read. Your support with revision will help students communicate clearly with readers and achieve their thematic purposes.

Communicate clearly

When you confer with students face-to-face, you can be more specific about why you feel a spot in the text needs to be revised. You can also suggest a few possibilities so that students can experiment with your idea or come up with something completely different. Don't be surprised if some students resubmit their drafts with minimal revision effort. Figure 2.13 shows an example of Nara's response to a request for a snapshot in her text.

Communicate to students that although they don't have to entertain your specific suggestion, something has to happen at that point in the text. At one point in my work with Nara, I reviewed the importance of showing, not telling in our fiction writing. She was tenacious, but so was I. If students struggle with, or react negatively to, revision suggestions, don't give

```
    Then I burst in.  "Amarilla!" she exclaimed
nervously. "What a surprise to see you."
    I started yelling insults at her.
How 'bout a snapshot of this scene?
    Nah!
```

Figure 2.13 When suggestions are phrased as questions, get ready for students' answers. It would have been better to be direct with this writer by commenting, "Add a snapshot here."

up. Leaving your suggestion in the text will give it time to percolate in the writer's mind. Recognize that editing is emotional work and great ideas don't just appear in a heartbeat. Just like Roald Dahl, students may get testy about revisions. As their editor, you need to accept that you might not get everything you ask for. Maintain your cheer and be respectful of the writer. Through conversation about a range of revision possibilities, you can help to make sure that the writer is as satisfied as you are with

Time
to
pop!

how the text has been developed. Respond with enthusiasm when students work through revision suggestions and produce creative solutions where you've indicated there might be a problem with the text.

Recognize that you're helping students develop a piece of writing that they can be proud of. Nara and I passed her story back and forth several times. Sometimes I convinced her of the need for a change. At other times, she convinced me that her way worked. On our final round of revisions, I could tell it was time to wrap it up. In response to a new suggestion, Nara wrote to me, "Don't give me another suggestion! You gave me like one million (no offense) suggestions. I'm exasperated." I wasn't offended at all by Nara's comment. I was amused by her frankness, appreciative of her hard work, and sensitive to the importance of taking responsibility for keeping our relationship positive and productive. It was time to publish *The Ten Year Memory* and get it out to her readers. In the end, Nara was proud of her text and so was I. In her author's note, she wrote that she believed that her story could help readers deal with the problem of exclusion. Our work mirrored the productive relationship of authors working with their editors—challenging, satisfying, symbiotic.

Like an editor, the classroom teacher is faced with the task of working with writers in publishing projects. Learning from editors, we can take up a more active role in our writing classrooms. As we do so, we must take on the responsibility for making the working relationship successful. We can enjoy the challenge of helping a writer shape and enact her vision for her text. Our working relationships with student writers will involve tensions and will require tact. Each relationship will be different but all relationships will benefit from respecting the intentions of the writer and having real conversations with students about their texts.

Improving Texts

Advocating for Student Writing

Daniel was considered a struggling learner at the beginning of third grade. He avoided reading and writing and preferred to draw during writing workshop, often creating elaborate pictures of explosions in his writer's notebook. Energetic, he worked quickly on all assignments and was often the first to finish. Over the course of the year, Daniel became more excited about reading and writing. A favorite writing topic was his father, and he loved to write about their fishing trips. He also was an animated participant in conversations about the books we discussed at reading workshop.

Daniel's rough drafts usually needed a lot of revision. I had to ask him to read his texts aloud to me to clarify what he had written. When I gave him suggestions, Daniel revised cheerfully but he very rarely revised his texts on his own. At times, I worried that I was helping him too much. I knew revision was important, but I was concerned about crossing some kind of line with my suggestions. Where I worried about Nara ignoring my suggestions, with Daniel I worried that I was too involved. Learning about editors and their work helped me to calm down and carry on. I learned that every text, just like every writer, is different. There's no set protocol for revising. When editors commit to working with a text, the work is intensive, creative, and ultimately helps students see their texts in new ways.

Writing Research: Treating Text like Clay

Writing process research brought a respectful shift to the ways writers and their texts were treated within writing classrooms. Student writers were able to choose their topics. Student texts were shared and shaped through multiple drafts and

writing conferences. During conferences, teachers learned to maintain a respectful distance from the text, listening and asking questions, rather than offering specific suggestions. Writing workshop became a place where students behaved like real authors, with greater choice and control over their texts.

As a writing teacher new to writing process, the emphasis on student selection of topics made teaching writing an especially engaging time for my students and for me. Over the years, however, I began to notice a lack of originality and energy in the texts students produced. I read countless texts about birthday parties, trips to amusement parks, new bicycles, family pets. Many students rewrote favorite television or video game scenes. At times, these stories contained examples of stereotypes and bias. Unless a text was blatantly violent or insulting, I usually respected the author's choices in their writing and accepted the text for publication. Over the years, I wondered why reading workshop had such a different energy compared to our writing workshop. Students passionately debated and discussed powerful themes and events highlighted in the books we were reading together, but their spirited intensity did not carry over into their writing (Heffernan 2004). Working in elementary classrooms, SooHoo and Brown (1994) also observed a disparity between the passion students demonstrated during their morning meeting discussions, and the flat and lifeless texts they wrote in writing workshop. Their students:

> wrote about . . . things they thought would make good stories. They drew their inspiration from a shared culture, not the one cultivated in the classroom community, but the one they shared as nine and ten year olds in Cerritos: the culture of Nintendo, X-men, and the Baby-Sitters Club. These were the story topics of choice. (100)

Donald Graves acknowledged the pull of social forces on student writers who rewrite stories from favorite television shows and movies during writing workshop and believed this trend can shift when students learn that their own lives offer up important topics (1994, 58).

For writing process researchers, student texts are rough drafts that will improve and change through revision. This emphasis on revision comes with cautions for teachers to respect student ownership of their stories, to ask questions, and to be good listeners (Lane 1993, 127; Calkins 1994, 227). Though revision is valued as an essential part of process writing, teachers are often discouraged from offering specific suggestions for changing texts.

I gained more confidence and got more involved with revising student texts when I read the work of critical writing researcher Barbara Kamler. For Kamler, stories are malleable constructions; they're made and can be "remade and rewritten" (2001, 177–78). Revision does not have to represent highly charged high stakes for our writers. It's important to remember that we are not revising the writer when we revise a text and we can and should get more involved with revision assistance. By treating a text like clay, we show the writer how to strengthen a text's impact on readers. Significant revision requires teacher intervention with student texts, not from the front of the room and not from notes written in margins, but through "clay work," which involves "more active engagement with the student on the page." Kamler revises with student writers, not only helping them to modify their ideas, but exploring alternative meanings to their texts with them as well (91).

Writing researchers all agree that revision is important. Although some encourage teachers to hold off on getting overly involved, others see the benefits of a more hands-on approach. Significant involvement is typical of how real authors work with their editors to revise their work. When we want to get more involved with student revision, we can look to the ways that editors approach revision of texts during the publication journey.

Learning from Editors: Making the Text the Best It Can Be

Most editors aren't specifically concerned with a writer's process, and their primary goal is not to help the writer develop skills to become a better writer in the future. Although some editors hope they contribute to the skills of the writer, the primary focus of the editor is the text itself as she works with the writer toward the goal of publishing. To do her job well, an editor *must* make suggestions that lead the writer toward improving the manuscript.

Before revising can begin, an editor must determine if a text fits into the *list* or *line* of the publishing house. Publishers release a limited number of books each year, and though large publishing firms tend to have lists that are more eclectic, smaller presses tailor their lists to more specific purposes. In addition to determining whether a text fits into the house's list, an editor checks other published texts to make sure the topic hasn't saturated the market. Though market trends do influence acquisitions, editors also rely on their personal tastes and initial reactions when selecting texts. Gerald Gross contends that although authorial intent must be honored, the integrity of the editor should also be taken into account when analyzing manuscripts: "If I had to work on a manuscript that was violently in opposition to everything I stood for and believed in, I . . . couldn't do a good job for the author. . . . Remember that there will always be someone to publish what you have walked away from" (1993, xvii).

Once a manuscript is accepted by a publisher, the editor temporarily shares responsibility for the text as it's revised. An editor "owes his first loyalty to the book" and becomes an advocate for the text as it moves toward publication (O'Shea Wade 1993, 78). Though a text ultimately belongs to the writer, Gross thinks of the text as "leased" to the editor during the publishing process (1993, xvi). Curtis claims that the editor's job involves a certain closeness to texts that we don't read about in literature for writing teachers:

> *It takes as much courage to love a book, in many ways, as it does to love a person, and sometimes there is as much at stake. But there can be no love without responsibility and no responsibility without fortitude.* (1993, 36)

Editing work is slow, creative, and intellectually challenging, and editors don't edit for editing's sake, but expect their work to lead to an improved text. Betsy Lerner claims that editing "requires a kind of deep immersion, a total concentration, and the best among us average five to ten pages an hour" (2000, 212). Waxman believes an editor "must train himself to read uncomfortably, to nag, to question, to probe, not to give the author the benefit of the doubt" (1993, 155). In an example of "extreme editing," Waxman describes working on texts with organizational problems:

> *Occasionally I have had to go through a chapter paragraph by paragraph, noting the subject of each one in the margin; once that was done, I photocopied the original and cut the copy apart, clipping all the paragraphs on the same subject together and then reorganizing the paragraphs.* (1993, 160)

Like teachers, most editors read texts after hours, in the evenings and on weekends (Williams 1993, 7; Friedman 1993, 288). They assume that most, if not all, revision suggestions will result in revisions by the author. Faith Sale writes, "If I'm doing my job properly every point I make should cause the author at least to think, if not to act" (1993, 270).

As a critical reader, the editor works as a mediator of sorts, readying the text to enter the reader's world. When editor Wendy Lamb reads a text, she gathers information to let the author know "where I am distracted, bored, confused, or where I don't believe in the world of the story. Ideally, the reader should never have an opportunity to doubt or turn away from the story" (Curtis and Lamb n.d.).

Editors keep the author's intentions in mind but stay open to possible new interpretations and meanings that can be developed (Williams 1993, 6). Schuster (1993) counsels fellow editors to not "pass judgment on a manuscript *as it is*, but *as it can be made to be*" (24).

When Sale edits fictional texts, authors sometimes argue against revising specific episodes because these episodes are based on events that occurred in real life. Sale counters that it doesn't matter if an episode is an actual experience of the writer. If the episode does not work in the text, it shouldn't be there (1993, 270). Some writers get overly attached to their texts and can't face making changes. Others go overboard with revision and don't know when to stop. The editor's job is one that friends and family cannot be relied upon to complete—"namely to read every line with care, to comment in detail with absolute candor, and to suggest changes where they seem desirable or even essential" (Williams 1993, 6).

Every new text requires a sense of commitment and represents a unique endeavor. Editors don't follow a set protocol for revising, even when they work with authors on many publications over time. Of her editing work with Steven Kellogg, Phyllis Fogelman writes: "Steven Kellogg and I have worked on twenty-seven books together. . . . Steven is a wonderful writer and illustrator and many of his books have gone easily and quickly. . . . With others, the process has been more complicated" (1993, 313).

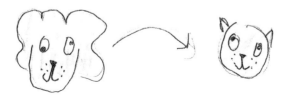

Though editors don't adhere to a uniform procedure or set of steps when revising a text, there are certain tenets they follow that can guide us when our students submit their drafts.

- Editors work for publishing houses. They *accept manuscripts that fit in with the list* of their press. Although some presses publish a wide range of texts, smaller presses frequently have a more focused publication list.

- Editing is challenging and creative work. Editors support the author's intentions, and they also *promote new meanings* during the revision process. When editors work with a text, their interpretations, as well as the writer's, guide the text along its long road toward publication.

- Editors *make substantive suggestions* to texts. Their suggestions can bring significant changes to a manuscript. They read to help the author revise the text in a plethora of ways.

The intense and creative commitment that editors make to the revision process should have a more prominent place in our writing workshops. From editors we can learn to gain confidence as we get more involved with student texts. "An editor has to be selfless," says Robert Gottlieb, "and yet also has to be strong minded. If you don't know what you think, or if you're nervous about expressing your opinion, what good is that to a writer?" (Lerner 2000, 218–19). Editors take responsibility for helping authors improve their texts. Publishing the best text possible is an obligation editors take seriously.

Teacher as Editor: Making Big Changes During Revision Work

When we become teacher–editors in our classroom presses, we get closer to student texts, making bold revision suggestions. Texts represent high stakes and we publish fewer texts with more intentionality. All presses are associated with their unique lists of publications. We familiarize students with which texts are a good fit for our lists so they know what kinds of texts to submit for publication. When we accept student texts for publication, we make a commitment to working closely with the text and becoming its advocate. Although the text ultimately belongs to the author, we stop worrying so much about ownership as we revise. We make a commitment to develop multiple meanings and to help the writer make his text the best it can be.

Some established presses have eclectic lists, publishing a wide range of books; smaller, independent presses tend to have a more specialized focus. An author wouldn't send a graphic novel to a press that publishes cookbooks and vice versa. Authors become familiar with the lists of various presses before submitting manuscripts to make sure their texts will be a good fit.

Classroom presses can be eclectic, publishing a wide range of genre. Or, they may have a more specific publishing focus. As I've become more committed to critical literacy pedagogy, Popcorn Press has evolved to feature texts that raise awareness about fairness and social action. This focus does not preclude an adherence to the district's curricular guidelines. As in most schools, students compose narrative, informational, and persuasive texts each year. But despite curricular mandates, social themes can be highlighted and developed in narratives, research reports, and persuasive essays. Regardless of the goals of the classroom press, there are three guiding questions to keep in mind when working with students to revise their texts:

- Does the text fit into the list of the classroom press?

- Can new ideas be developed?

- How can this text be revised to make it the best it can be?

History Trail: Inspiring Student Writers Through Mentor Texts

Teachers have always used favorite mentor texts to model examples of great writing and generate conversation around powerful themes in literacy workshops. Mentor texts can also serve as representations of the kinds of books we aim to publish in the classroom press. After reading and discussing texts, we post salient pictures or passages from the texts on a bulletin board, which we call the History Trail (Harste and Vasquez 1998, 273). Our trail contains a sampling of the texts—picture books, photographs, news articles—that generated conversations about fairness throughout the school year. We use these books as writing workshop resources as well, using the revision template to identify important themes, messages, and examples of fine writer's craft. (See Figure 3.1.)

Text	Themes
Crow Boy (Yashima 1976)	• Don't tease. • Kindness should be a law. • Don't leave anybody behind.
The Girl with 500 Middle Names (Haddix 2001)	• Keep promises. • Money's not everything. • You don't have to have fancy clothes.
Harvesting Hope (Krull 2003)	• People are not tools. Don't treat them like tools. • The farm workers marched to protest their working conditions. • Find out how your food gets to the supermarket.
Augustino Nieves Testimony (Nieves 2002)	• Families stick together. • Children shouldn't be hired for jobs. • Six years old is too young to work. • No child labor.
Coolies (Yin 2001)	• Equal rights! • Railroad workers are people too! • Hard work for little pay is not fair.
Carpet Boy's Gift (Shea 2003) *Fight for Child Workers!* (Cremin 2002)	• Kids should not work. Kids should only do chores. • Don't make kids work. Is money more important than kids? • Only adults should work in factories.
By These Hands (Parker 2002)	• Make work visible! • We work hard! • Don't stereotype workers!
Gleam and Glow (Bunting 2001)	• Do not burn homes. • War hurts kids. • Two fish can make a difference in the world. • Sometimes you have to have hope.
Voices in the Park (Browne 1998)	• You can play with whomever you want. • Boys and girls should be able to be friends.
The Bobbin Girl (McCully 1996)	• Have hope in the world. • Workers want equal pay! • People are not machines!

Figure 3.1 A chart shows the list of our History Trail bulletin board books and the important themes the class identified.

A representation of our classroom life together, the History Trail also becomes an important source of inspiration for student writers, helping students identify themes and topics they care about. History Trail texts bookmark our conversations, but also provide great examples of powerful writing in a range of genre. We can point out to our students that all of the authors represented on the History Trail had editors helping them revise and publish their texts. Instead of announcing, "I wish I had written this book!" after reading a text to my students, I now say, "I wish I had published this book. It's a great fit for our press!"

Each year the History Trail has a different look and feel to it. Students get interested in different themes as the texts take us in different directions. The year Daniel was in my class, we talked quite a bit about work and worker's rights. Our History Trail featured texts such as *Harvesting Hope* (Krull 2003), *Coolies* (Yin 2001), *By These Hands* (Parker 2002), *The Carpet Boy's Gift* (Shea 2003), and *The Bobbin Girl* (McCully 1996). As we discussed the stories about work and laborers, we also talked about stereotypes—how some work comes to be known as men's work and some comes to be known as women's work. Janet shared at morning meeting that she saw a *Men at Work* sign on her drive to school, and then noticed that one of the construction workers was a woman. Students noticed different ways stereotypical assumptions are made about people, based on gender. Our classroom conversations later make their way into the writing students do, as they discover ideas and themes that interest them.

Making a Commitment to Revising Texts

Every classroom press—and every History Trail—will be unique, according to the goals for the publishing we want to do with students. Students can use the History Trail to incorporate important themes into their writing, but it's not a requirement. In Daniel's class, about half the students wrote about the theme of work when it came time to write fiction stories that year. The rest of the class chose different themes. Nara wrote about bullying. Janet wrote on an environmental theme, focusing on characters trying to stop a nearby forest from being cut down. Daniel combined two History Trail themes in his story, entitled *A Dangerous Job*. Daniel's theme was stereotyping workers (see Figure 3.2). He wanted readers to know that workers are sometimes stereotyped and not treated with respect. Daniel looked over the

History Trail as well as his notebook entries when he began thinking about writing his fiction story.

Our press publishes stories with surprising and powerful themes. Daniel's theme fit the criteria, so I agreed that his story would be a good fit for our classroom press and he began writing. First he planned his story with a storyboard, using six sticky notes to design the main events in his story (Figure 3.3).

Daniel wrote one page for each sticky note. He skipped lines and only wrote on the front side of each page. As usual, Daniel was the first student to complete his

Name_____ Date_____

Picture Book Project

Crow Boy
Gleam and Glow
Harvesting Hope
Bobbin Girl
Coolies
PowerPoint Presentations

PURPOSE: We've read some powerful books with some big themes. We've had amazing conversations about our connections. Now it's time to write a book that will influence readers and help people think about the world.

Look through your notebook entries.

Do any pieces stand out to you? Put a sticker next to any sections that seem especially interesting and original.

If you have explored any big themes in your writing, write them at the top of your page.

How can you include some of your notebooks entries to write a picture book that will make your readers have a big conversation?

Share your theme pieces with a learning partner.

****

Picture Book Proposal:

I want to write about this theme: Sterotype workers.

I will use   2   notebook entries from my packet.

My book will be: (fiction)   non-fiction

Figure 3.2 The History Trail becomes a starting point for writers choosing themes for their stories.

Figure 3.3 Sticky note storyboarding gives students a flexible outline for beginning their stories. It also helps when you confer with writers about the trajectories of their stories.

fiction story. After his six pages were done, he proofread his story with red pencil, finding and fixing twenty-three writing errors. He then used the revision template to read through his story to revise his ideas and elements of craft. Daniel made very few revisions on his story before submitting it. *A Dangerous Job* is about a father who gets injured at work.

> *One blazing day me and my friends were playing with our remote control cars. Suddenly my mom came screaming. George your father got hurt. He fell out of his crane and broke his leg and arm. Frantically his friend Robert came over and we waited.*
>
> *George's dad fell off the crane. He felt as if he was jumping into an eight-foot pool and he hit his head but luckily he had a hard hat on his head. So he tipped over and broke his right arm and leg. He heard sirens loud as a lion's roar calling for him.*
>
> *As my mom told me to get the fire ready and she dropped me off and I got the wood and the matches and lit the fire and it exploded and we cooked marshmallows.*

When we receive manuscripts from our students, it's easy to be a bit disappointed at first. We work so hard planning and teaching our minilessons and when students hand in their rough drafts, their writing often seems so . . . well . . . rough.

I found Daniel's story to be quite confusing and wondered how the plot connected to his theme. Our classroom press publishes books that are well written, original, surprising, and powerful. Though I didn't feel his story was well written *yet*, Daniel had created an original story and I felt I could help him make it more powerful. Like authors whose books were featured on our History Trail, Daniel was inspired to explore the difficulties faced by people whose daily work involves dangerous hazards. His exuberance for our class conversations about *Coolies*, *The Bobbin Girl*, and *The Carpet Boy's Gift* came through in his choice of theme and plot. I could also see that Daniel had integrated ideas from his writer's notebook by focusing on a father-son relationship in *A Dangerous Job*.

Daniel's manuscript fit well with the list of Popcorn Press. I was eager to help him get this text shaped up and into the hands of readers. I also anticipated that his story would require some extreme editing.

Developing New Ideas Through Revision

Daniel's story is about a construction worker who is also a dad. The story begins at home, where a young boy, George, plays with friends. Play time is interrupted when George's mom delivers the bad news that his father's been hurt at work. A friend joins George at home and they wait for more news. The story shifts to the construction site where we see the father fall from a vehicle and lay injured on the ground, waiting for an ambulance. The ending involves another scene change, where we see George preparing a fire. Reunited, the family cooks marshmallows together.

When I accepted Daniel's manuscript, I made a commitment to his text. Normally, I would type the draft and embed my suggestions into the text, but Daniel had handed in an incomplete revision template (see Figure 2.8, page 31) with his story. The Meaning Making section of the template is the place where students write down two or three ideas readers might consider as they read the text. Daniel didn't fill in this section, but that didn't worry me. Some writers need help with it, and the template is often a supportive tool for conferences with students. I used the template as the basis of my writing conference with Daniel. After clarifying some confusing parts, we turned our attention to the template and thought about ideas he wanted to get across to readers:

> **Lee:** I have a few questions for you before I start typing. What kind of work does the father do? I know it's some kind of construction, right?
>
> **Daniel:** He's making a road. Bombing out a road.
>
> **Lee:** Got it. And what about the fire at the end?
>
> **Daniel:** They're having a cookout.
>
> **Lee:** Is the dad at home at the end?
>
> **Daniel:** Yeah, he came home in the ambulance.
>
> **Lee:** OK, sounds good. Let's think about what you really want readers to know or understand. This helps me when I'm typing up your story and making suggestions.
>
> **Daniel:** I wasn't sure what to write there. (*Pointing to the revision template*)
>
> **Lee:** No worries. That's why we're having this conference. I want to make sure your thoughts and ideas are clear to your readers. If someone reads your story, what would they get from it?

Daniel: "His leg got caught in the conveyor."

Lee: So you're saying construction work is dangerous? [*Notice how I rephrase what he said to convey a big idea.*]

Daniel: Yeah. Anything can happen at any time.

Lee: Why don't you write that down? That's an important part of your story. OK, based on our History Trail work, your story reminds me of something else that could be interesting to include. Remember when the character in *Coolies* got hurt and couldn't work? The dad in your story might not be able to work for a while. When that happens today, people get worker's compensation. Do you know what that is?

Daniel: No.

Lee: Well, it's money that workers receive when they get hurt on the job. A teacher I knew once got hurt at work. She kicked a soccer ball at recess and fell and hurt her back. She got something called *worker's compensation*. That means she received her salary while she was healing. A lot of teachers and workers belong to unions and the union helps protect their rights.

Daniel (*Looking confused*): So what do you want me to write here?

Lee: Well. Maybe something like . . . workers who get hurt. . . .

Daniel: Can get money?

Lee: That could work. Let's keep thinking about that.

Daniel: I think of things, but I don't write them down.

Lee: It's OK not to write down everything you think of. I was also wondering about George. How is he feeling in this story? What are you trying to get readers to think about through George's story?

Daniel (*Writing quickly*): Kids should be worried about their dad's job.

Lee: Really? Most people think parents should be worried about kids, not the other way around.

Daniel: That's not the way I see it.

Lee: So you feel *all* kids should worry about parents?

Daniel (*Emphatically*): Yes!

During our conference, we talked about different ideas for Daniel's story—construction work is dangerous, worker's compensation, and how kids should worry about their parents. It's clear that Daniel wasn't overjoyed with my suggestion about bringing worker's compensation into his story, but I thought it could fit well with his text. Most of the books on our History Trail were historical fiction. In our conversations about these mentor texts, we had touched upon the rights that are now part of workers' lives because of the labor movement. I was happy that we ended our conference with ideas Daniel was excited about. His comment about kids worrying about parents was an original idea that would help him develop his main character as he revised his text. The back-and-forth revision partnership was on its way.

Making Substantive Revisions

Usually students have a go at revising their texts before they submit them to me. With red pencil, Daniel had corrected over twenty problems with conventions—missing capitals, punctuation, fixing a few run-on sentences. He also circled some powerful words and phrases, *frantically* and *loud as a lion's roar*, with an orange pencil, indicating that he had paid attention to the Writer's Craft section of the template. The template helps me organize my thoughts as I suggest revisions to students. As I read a text, I ask three types of questions:

- **Meaning:** Do all parts of this story make sense? Are any sections unnecessary or repetitive? Which ideas will stand out to future readers?

- **Craft:** Does the lead hook the reader? Does the ending leave the reader thinking? Could the author add any powerful words or more descriptive details?

- **Theme:** Is the author's theme coming across? Can any new themes or social issues be explored in greater depth?

Daniel needed to elaborate his story in several spots. His ending was abrupt. What was going to happen to the father? Was he permanently disabled because of his fall? Could he still work? The story seemed to be just beginning. As we passed the text back and forth, I made revision suggestions in the areas of meaning, craft, and themes:

Revising for Meaning

- Show the physical consequences of the injury. What actually happened?

- Create a scene where George's dad argues with his boss about worker's compensation.

- Add dialogue that shows George's concern for his dad. Add scenes where the characters interact.

Revising for Craft

- Lead: Switch the first two scenes. Open with more of a snapshot of George and his friend.

- Snapshots: Add a snapshot of the actual injury. Add descriptive details about the cookout scene.

- Ending: Extend the story so we know the consequences of the dad's accident. Have George and his father playing cars together at the end to show things will be OK.

Revising for Social Awareness and Action

- Add another construction worker character that reports the injury. This character could be a woman to show readers that construction workers are men and women.

- Add a scene where George defends his dad and his job, speaking up when a friend makes disparaging remarks.

Daniel's story required extreme editing. I offered suggestions that focused on the text. We passed the story back and forth between us, sometimes working together, sometimes working separately. When I made suggestions in the draft, I left spaces for Daniel to revise (see Figure 3.4).

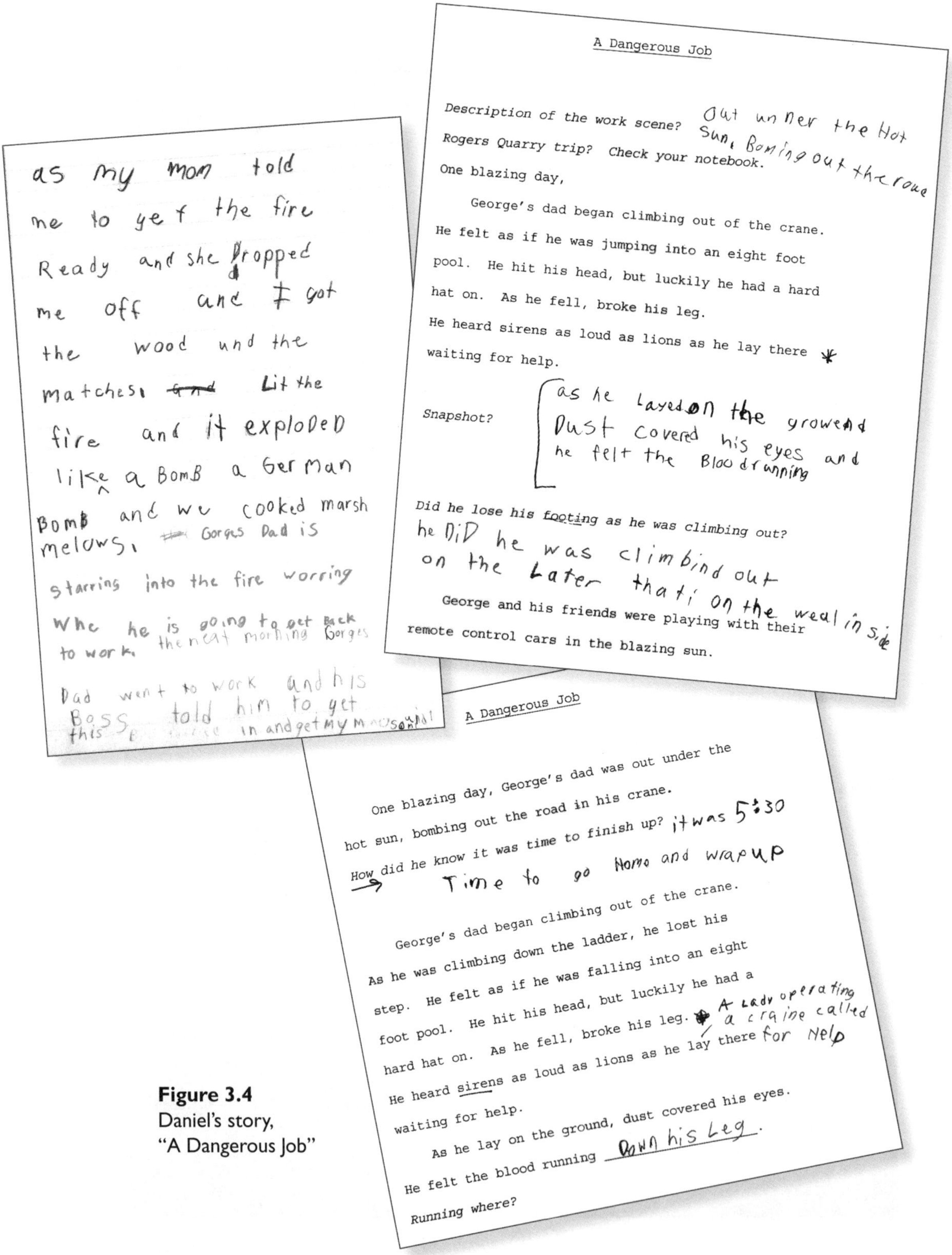

First draft (left paper)

as my mom told me to get the fire Ready and she Dropped me off and I got the wood and the matches, ~~and~~ Lit the fire and it exploDeD like a BomB a GerMan BomB and we cooked marsh melows. ~~Here~~ Gorges Dad is starring into the fire worring whe he is going to get Back to work. the next morning Gorges Dad went to work and his Boss told him to get this ~~e~~ in and get my mousanyal

Middle paper

A Dangerous Job

Description of the work scene? Out un Ner the Hot Sun, Boming out the road

Rogers Quarry trip? Check your notebook.

One blazing day,

George's dad began climbing out of the crane. He felt as if he was jumping into an eight foot pool. He hit his head, but luckily he had a hard hat on. As he fell, broke his leg.

He heard sirens as loud as lions as he lay there ✳ waiting for help.

Snapshot?

⌈as he layed on the growend Dust Covered his eyes and he felt the Blood running

Did he lose his footing as he was climbing out?

he DiD he was climbind out on the Later that on the weal inside

George and his friends were playing with their remote control cars in the blazing sun.

Bottom paper

A Dangerous Job

One blazing day, George's dad was out under the hot sun, bombing out the road in his crane. How did he know it was time to finish up? it was 5:30

→ Time to go Home and wrap up

George's dad began climbing out of the crane. As he was climbing down the ladder, he lost his step. He felt as if he was falling into an eight foot pool. He hit his head, but luckily he had a hard hat on. As he fell, broke his leg. ✳ A Lady operating a craine called for Help

He heard sirens as loud as lions as he lay there waiting for help.

As he lay on the ground, dust covered his eyes. He felt the blood running Down his Leg.

Running where?

Figure 3.4
Daniel's story,
"A Dangerous Job"

A Dangerous Job

One blazing day, George's dad was out under the hot sun, bombing out the road in his crane. It was 5:30. Time to wrap up and go home.

George's dad began climbing out of the crane. As he was climbing down the ladder, he lost his step. He felt as if he was falling into an eight foot pool. He hit his head, but luckily he had a hard hat on. As he fell, he broke his leg. As he lay on the ground, dust covered his eyes. He felt the blood running down his leg. A woman operating a crane nearby called on her radio for help. He heard sirens as loud as lions as he lay there waiting.

Back at home, George and his friends were playing with their remote control cars in the blazing sun out on the sidewalk. As the sun was setting, George felt like he was sitting on the blue flames of a fire.

George's family was going to have a cookout that evening. Suddenly George's mom came out of the house screaming, "George, your father got hurt. He tripped getting out of the crane and got his leg stuck in the tread. He broke his leg."

George didn't know what to say. His friend asked, "Why doesn't your dad get a desk job? It's a lot safer!"

George got mad. "My dad likes his job. He's in a good position."

"Sorry, don't bite my head off."

George said, "Don't make fun of my dad. If you do, you can go home."

Frantic, George and his friends waited for more news. After a few hours, an ambulance pulled into the driveway. Dad walked by himself out of the ambulance. He had both a cane and a crutch. He was hunched over like a lion ready to pounce as he walked out.

continues

Figure 3.4 *continued*

Mom told George to get the fire ready. George got the wood and the matches. He lit the fire and it exploded.

As George cooked marshmallows, his dad stared into the fire. He was worrying about when he could get back to work. George asked his dad to tell the story of how he got hurt. So he told him.

The next morning, George's dad went to work and his boss told him to go home. But George's dad said, "I'll sit here all day if I have to. I'll call the union if I have to. I need to get worker's compensation for this injury."

The boss said, "I'll get your check."

"I'll be back in two weeks," said Dad. Then he went home.

He walked into the kitchen and looked out the window. He saw George walking back and forth, back and forth. Dad went and got his old remote control cars. He went outside to see George.

"Want to play cars with me, George?" He was holding a car in his hand. "I'll be home for a few weeks, but then I'll be back to work. Everything's going to be okay."

"Sure Dad," said George, "I'll play." He hugged his dad and they set up the cars together.

Figure 3.4 *continued*

Often, he would come and ask me to explain some of my suggestions. When I suggested a change, I expected that Daniel would at least consider it and usually he was eager to try his hand at taking his text in new directions. Daniel loved talking about possibilities for his story and was proud to share his final draft (see Figure 3.5) with other writers in our classroom.

My work with Daniel led to significant revisions of his story. The work is more intensive and text focused than my revision work with students in the past, but it also

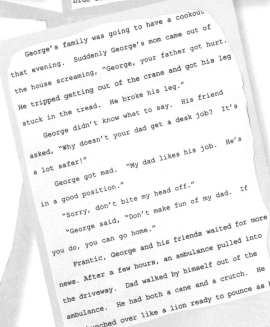

A Dangerous Job

One blazing day, George's dad was out under the hot sun, bombing out the road in his crane. It was 5:30. Time to wrap up and go home.

George's dad began climbing out of the crane. As he was climbing down the ladder, he lost his step. He felt as if he was falling into an eight foot pool. He hit his head, but luckily he had a hard hat on. As he fell, he broke his leg. As he lay on the ground, dust covered his eyes. He felt the blood running down his leg. A woman operating a crane nearby called on her radio for help. He heard sirens as loud as lions as he lay there waiting.

Back at home, George and his friends were playing with their remote control cars in the blazing sun out on the sidewalk. As the sun was setting, George felt like he was sitting on the blue flames of a fire.

George's family was going to have a cookout that evening. Suddenly George's mom came out of the house screaming, "George, your father got hurt. He tripped getting out of the crane and got his leg stuck in the tread. He broke his leg."

George didn't know what to say. His friend asked, "Why doesn't your dad get a desk job? It's a lot safer!"

George got mad. "My dad likes his job. He's in a good position."

"Sorry, don't bite my head off."

George said, "Don't make fun of my dad. If you do, you can go home."

Frantic, George and his friends waited for more news. After a few hours, an ambulance pulled into the driveway. Dad walked by himself out of the ambulance. He had both a cane and a crutch. He was hunched over like a lion ready to pounce as he walked out.

Figure 3.5 Daniel's story, "A Dangerous Job"

continues

Mom told George to get the fire ready. George got the wood and the matches. He lit the fire and it exploded like a bomb.

As George cooked marshmallows, his dad stared into the fire. He was worrying about when he could get back to work. George asked his dad to tell the story of how he got hurt. So he told him.

The next morning, George's dad went to work and his boss told him to go home. But George's dad said, "I'll sit here all day if I have to. I'll call the union if I have to. I need to get worker's compensation for this injury."

The boss said, "I'll get your check."

"I'll be back in two weeks," said Dad. Then he went home.

He walked into the kitchen and looked out the window. He saw George walking back and forth, back and forth. Dad went and got his old remote control cars. He went outside to see George.

"Want to play cars with me, George?" He was holding a car in his hand. "I'll be home for a few weeks, but then I'll be back to work. Everything's going to be okay."

"Sure Dad," said George, "I'll play." He hugged his dad and they set up the cars together.

Author's Note

I wrote this story to show that kids should worry about their parents. When they get hurt. Like the dad in this story. My story shows that people can be stereotyped in all different ways.

Figure 3.5 *continued*

brings a new level of engagement with revision targeted on Daniel's specific writing strengths and struggles. Working as his editor, I helped Daniel develop his skills in four areas—learning proofreading conventions, developing a wider range of meanings or purposes for his story, crafting a story creatively, and pursuing social justice aims for his text. While helping him improve his current text in these ways, I was also helping him develop skills that he will use in the future.

Many teachers already use writing templates or rubrics to assess student writing. The Four Reads Revision Template works as a formative assessment. Daniel had a good handle on two key elements of craft. He included figurative language and power words in his writing. He needed help crafting his lead and ending. During orange read conferences, we looked through the mentor texts from our History Trail to see different possibilities for his lead. He was especially intrigued by the lead of *Harvesting Hope*, the story about Cesar Chavez. In contrast, he needed some coaching with the green read. By talking to him about what he wanted a reader to take away from his story, we were able to work together to broaden and complicate his plot. Once these purposes were clearer, we could work together on developing them in the text. Working concretely, with the text in hand, an editor reflects on what a text needs. The needs of the text connect to the needs of the writer.

An editor's perspective allows us to draw on our own creativity when working with writers to publish final drafts that are significantly different from rough drafts. We publish fewer texts each year, but we have greater intentionality about the texts we publish. Though there are more back-and-forth interactions around texts, we give up some of the stress around revision that we may have experienced in our classrooms in the past. We can lighten up about who owns the text. We can lighten up about being too bossy when we expect that our suggestions lead our students to make significant changes to texts. We can lighten up about helping students too much. When students need help with revisions, we can offer suggestions freely, knowing that editors in publishing houses give published authors just this kind of professional assistance. Acting as an editor, we can give our students and their texts the same kind of attention that published authors get from their editors.

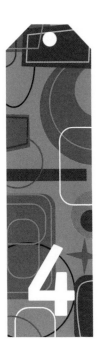

Connecting with Readers

Being Mindful of Purpose and Audience

At our end of the year portfolio conference, I asked Daniel, "Why'd you write your story, 'A Dangerous Job'?"

He answered, "I just . . . I felt like I should write this book 'cause out of all the stories this is the one that probably will make kids change their life. Turn their life around." I asked him to say more about that, and he added, "I think after someone reads it, he'll realize, man . . . I really don't pay attention to my dad that much."

I asked Daniel if anyone else in the class had written anything similar. He emphatically answered, "Nope. There's nothing else like it."

Daniel believed that his story would be thought-provoking and even life changing for his readers. Even though his draft required extensive revision, his commitment to his theme had been strong throughout the publication journey. Not all students have this great sense of social purpose during their writing process.

Janet knew she wanted to write an adventure story, but she couldn't decide on a theme.

"Could a theme be *adventure*?" she asked.

I had reservations, but I decided to be flexible about this, because adventure stories frequently do explore big themes. I told Janet, "An adventure story could be good. You could weave a theme into it, right? Maybe your characters deal with some problems on their adventure?"

Janet said she was going to try that. She didn't know yet what the character's problem would be, but she was excited. A highly motivated student, Janet quickly made a sticky note storyboard and started to write. She filled up the six pages from her storyboard and kept going. She wrote for days. She couldn't stop. I was getting nervous, but I let her write on. I always tell students that the length of a story doesn't improve its impact, so I started getting a little nervous when after a few days, I heard a student announce in awe, "Janet has twenty-seven pages and she's still going!" When I noticed other students cheering her on as if she were a marathon runner, I decided it was probably time to check in with Janet. I asked her if she was close to finishing and she said, "Not even close." I asked her to turn in her draft that day so I could read it over.

After school, I read Janet's adventure story about a young girl who walks through the woods and finds a small cabin. She walks through the front door into a small room. Inside the room, she sees a chest of drawers. She opens a drawer and finds a wand. She then sees another door and walks through it. Guess what happens in the next room? More drawers. She opens a drawer and finds a map. The story continues on with various doors and drawers for twenty-five more pages. *Doors and Drawers* would have been the perfect title for this book. I felt badly that Janet had spent so much time on her book and vowed to stick to the guidelines I had set up for the press in the future. The manuscript had been tough reading. I could think of no other readers who would find the story interesting as it was presently written.

When I asked Janet at our writing conference where she was going with the book, how it was going to all end up, she shook her head. Looking frustrated, she shrugged, "I don't know."

I suggested that we look through her notebook for some possible themes that she cared about. I also apologized for abandoning her. I knew the guidelines helped students but I was still pulled by old perceptions that the writer should control the text. Even though our press had certain guidelines for authors, I had made an exception for Janet and left her to her own devices.

In her notebook, Janet had written a piece about a local wooded area that was going to be cut down for a housing development. Protests in our town had appeared in the newspaper several times and the class had discussed the situation at morning meeting. I asked Janet if she was interested

in having her characters do something to prevent a forest from being cut down. She liked the idea. Janet began writing a new story about kids taking action. After revisions were complete, Janet was pleased with her new story and so was I. Through her story, readers would get to know characters who could speak up and work together to make change. The new draft had a clear conflict and resolution as well as a strong environmental theme.

Sometimes writers get caught up in their writing and lose sight of the reader. This is natural, and it is why being an editor for our students is so important. Student publications can contribute to important conversations inside the classroom and out and can cause readers to think and act in new ways. Our students can come to see the power of writing to impact readers.

Writing Research: Student Writing Impacts Readers

Sometimes our students create texts just for themselves, recalling and recording their personal experiences, thoughts, and imaginings. When they write to share ideas or stories with readers, however, their writing has a more social purpose. Writing process researchers focus attention on the social purposes of writing by promoting increased audience for student writers. Before writing workshop became prevalent in elementary classrooms, teachers were the primary audience for student writing. Teachers read, graded, and then returned student texts. With writing workshop, students have multiple opportunities to share their texts—writing conferences, author's chair, and publishing celebrations. Student texts become part of the reading material available in classroom libraries.

Writing process researchers present writing as a form of communication, as well as an avenue for student writers to impact and influence readers. Our students learn to not only view writing as a way to "clarify their own thinking," but also as a "powerful tool they can use to influence others" (Graves 1994, 44). As they develop as active citizens, students should learn about, and experience, the power of writing to "command the attention of others" (45).

Because written communication plays such a critical role in our daily lives, student writers should have more awareness and intention about the power their writing can have. Critical writers can imagine "alternative arrangements for self and society" in their texts (Shor 1999, 20). Through writing, students can question social norms and stereotypes and can influence readers to do the same (Heffernan and Lewison 2003; Lensmire 2000; Clifford and Ervin 1999). Hardin writes that student writing has the potential for contributing to societal change. Even when student texts do not circulate outside the classroom, the critical writer is engaged in "real cultural work" (2001, 52–53).

Nancy Welch encourages teachers to use revision to increase student awareness of the impact writing can have on readers. Our revision suggestions help our students enact social goals with their texts (1997, 164–65). Through the revision relationship between teacher and student, students can learn how "individual stories join, disrupt, change, and are changed by the words of others" (120).

In my classroom, I found that when students explored social issues and themes in their stories, they came together as a group of writers who felt they were doing important work (Heffernan 2004). The social purposes that come with publishing can transform the writing workshop into a writer's collective, where writers come together with shared social purposes. Writing workshops can be a place for critical literacy, where students use writing to challenge dominant storylines and question the status quo (Kamler 2001, 73).

Writing researchers urge teachers to focus on the critical social purposes writing can have. Writing teachers should rethink not only what students are writing in classrooms, but what that writing can do out in the world (Kamler 2001, 173). Writing researchers show us that writing, even at the elementary level, can have impact on readers. It makes sense that writing teachers turn to the work of editors for guidance as we consider audience for student writing. Readership is part and parcel of the editor's job.

Learning from Editors: Commanding the Attention of Readers

Even though much of publishing is big business, editors continue to do the work of reading and making decisions about which manuscripts will be published and made

available to readers. Editor Betsy Lerner says, "Editors are still the world's readers and thus the eyes of the world" (2000, 207–208).

An editor reads a manuscript with future readers in mind. Inhabiting a unique place between authors and readers, editors make judgments and best guesses about who will read a text and for what purpose. Before accepting a manuscript, editors evaluate what a text can do in the world. They think about how a text fits into the market. Will there be readers for this book? Who might be interested in it?

Editors believe that the books they publish can make a difference in the world of readers. Curtis says editors must resist the "pressures toward homogeneity and mediocrity" that are part of corporate publishing (1993, 29). Schuster encourages his fellow editors to be trendsetters, rather than trend followers (1993, 25). Even in an industry that looks to increase and guarantee profits, Schuster believes that an editor's "greatest joy and highest privilege" comes from publishing books that meet societal needs that are "still unmet" (1993, 24). Howard contends that the corporatization of publishing has not eliminated the opportunity to publish "the risky, the new, the demanding work" (1993, 66).

Individual editors working with writers have had a huge impact on the types of children's literature available to young readers. The editor of Julius Lester's *To Be a Slave*, Fogelman believed that children's books have multiple functions; they not only "provide pleasure," they "can and should expand the imagination as well as foster knowledge and children's understanding of the world and the people in it" (1993, 307).

Commenting on Sendak's "revolutionary" *Where the Wild Things Are* (1963), editor Ursula Nordstrom writes, "Maurice's book is the first picture book to recognize the fact that children have powerful emotions, anger and love and hate" (Marcus 1998, 184). Nordstrom published many "first" books in her decades as lead editor at Harper Collins, books that brought topics such as homosexuality, menstruation, racism, and divorce into children's stories for the first time (Marcus 1998, 261).

Although larger presses usually publish eclectic lists, smaller independent presses frequently target specific niche markets of readers—people of specific ages, or readers with specific interests. Some presses aim to put out books that lead readers to reimagine the status quo or challenge social norms. Milkweed Press publishes books to make "a humane impact on society" (Pope 2005, 157). Tricycle Press seeks out books "outside the mainstream; books that encourage children to look at the world from a different angle" (Pope 2005, 193).

Because an editor gets to make choices about the books that eventually get into readers' hands, many claim they aim to stay mindful of the reasoning behind their decisions. Gross believes that he must stay true to his own convictions to be truly responsible to the author, the book, and the reader (1993, xvii). Editors have to consider both commerce and art (Silbersack 1993, 296), and they try to reconcile what sells with their own preferences and goals (298). Though editors use their expertise to make predictions about which texts will succeed with readers, they're ultimately relying on their best guesses and publishing is largely an experimental enterprise. A dozen publishing houses passed up *Harry Potter and the Philosopher's Stone* (1997) before an editor brought it home and shared it with his eight-year-old daughter.

Near retirement in 1980, Ursula Nordstrom imagined the creation of a new publishing company called Marginal Books, Inc., where she could ignore "the tiny tiny little persons who live on the well-known bottom line" (Marcus 1998, 372), and she pointed out that many of the marginal books she published became unpredicted successes and remain in print today. In addition to Sendak's books, Nordstrom edited beloved classics like *The Giving Tree* (Silverstein 1964), *William's Doll* (Zolotow 1972), and *Charlotte's Web* (White 1952). Considered by some reviewers to be unsuitable for young children, these books continue to find readers today. Author Charlotte Zolotow referred to Nordstrom as "one of the great innovators . . . She liked realistic books, where parents weren't always dear and good and children faced problems in their lives" (Anderson 1988).

Editors work with an eye to how a text will be received once it's out in the world. Though our students' writing doesn't always circulate far from our classrooms, teachers already resemble small press editors in many ways. Throughout the school year, we work closely with a group of writers on publishing projects and we revise with students so that their writing is reader friendly. Learning from editors, we can increase our students' sense that their writing can be a powerful way to influence and hold the attention of a reading audience.

- Editors keep the reader in mind during the publication journey. Editors look to publish work that's original and thought-provoking to impact readers. Editors make predictions about readership, but there are no guarantees and they recognize that their decisions are often based on their best guesses, rather than scientific principles.

- Many editors work intentionally to publish writing that disrupts or critiques the status quo. They aim to publish creative firsts that meet social needs not previously met. They've taken risks and published books that some considered revolutionary or controversial.

Editors think of books as social goods that meet particular social needs. Lad Tobin claims that part of an editor's job is learning to discipline the marketplace while being disciplined by it (1993, 365). When editors judge a book, they are also making judgments about who will read it. Readership is an essential component of an editor's job as they strive to publish texts that command the attention of the reading public.

Teacher as Editor: Helping Writers with Powerful Revisions

We can take up an editor stance in our classrooms without worrying about having to sell our students' writing or maximizing profits for our classroom presses. We don't have to produce best sellers, win awards, or garner great reviews from literary magazines. Without the pressure of the bottom line, we are free to be creative about how we approach issues of audience and readership with our students. During the back-and-forth of revision, we can discuss how readers might perceive and react to texts. Through our classroom presses, our students can publish original writing about ideas and issues kids care about, creating texts that are both interesting and important.

Before our students can publish texts that pack a punch, they need to know that writing is a powerful tool for communicating ideas and influencing readers. Even young writers should know that their publications can be influential and can set trends, rather than follow them. Not all the texts we publish are going to be "creative firsts" for readers, but they should at least be firsts for writers. Too often, students write repetitively, choosing the same topics over and over again. As we work with writers, we can keep an eye to readership. Like editors, we can ask ourselves:

- How can I help these writers best get their ideas across to readers?

- How can student texts bring original and thought-provoking ideas to future readers?

Exploring the Impact Writing Has on Readers

There's probably no more groundbreaking and influential book than Maurice Sendak's *Where the Wild Things Are*. This book changed children's literature forever. An added bonus of working with this book is that Maurice Sendak has spoken and written extensively about his relationship with his editor, Ursula Nordstrom. Explore the impact a single text can have on readers by shining light on the groundbreaking qualities of Sendak's classic text. Share your own memories of reading this book in the past and ask your students:

Have you ever read *Where the Wild Things Are*?

What do you remember about the story or the illustrations?

Who read it to you? How old were you when you first read it?

Have you read it more than once?

Read this classic book aloud, or any other favorite book that's had a lasting impact on children's literature. Students will probably be familiar with Sendak's book, but they may not know that this book elicited strong reactions from reviewers and readers and set trends in the world of children's literature. Share the following information in a book talk after your read-aloud.

Ursula Nordstrom was Sendak's editor. Many people don't know that this book was going to be called *Where the Wild Horses Are*, but Sendak was having difficulty. He didn't know how to draw horses. Nordstrom asked him, "What can you draw, Maurice?" Sendak replied, "Things."

And so, *Where the Wild Things Are* was born!

- When the book was published in 1963, people reacted strongly to it. Some reviewers thought the book was too scary for kids. Others thought that Max set a bad example for young readers with his misbehavior.

- Despite the controversy, it was nominated for, and won, the Caldecott Medal in 1964.

- The book has sold over twenty million copies and has been in print for over fifty years.

- After *Where the Wild Things Are* became popular, characters in children's books were portrayed in more complicated, more realistic ways.

Familiarize your students with book blurbs by sharing and discussing a few together. Point out that book blurbs contain a brief summary of the book, but mostly focus on a persuasive pitch to get readers interested. Students can then spend some time reading book blurbs from books in the classroom library. Have them keep an eye out for blurbs they find especially persuasive.

As a class, write a book blurb for *Where the Wild Things Are*. Your book blurb will be brief, but dramatic, giving a hint of a summary and showing the impact that the book had on you as a class of readers (Figure 4.1).

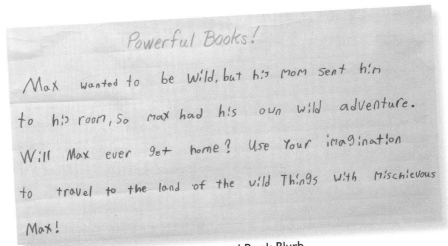

Figure 4.1 Example of a Class-Generated Book Blurb

If you have samples of student publications from past years, have students discuss the impact these books have had on them as readers. What seems important about the text? Which parts made them take notice or surprised them? Book blurbs are great, brief examples of the impact that a book can have on a reader. Have students write blurbs for books that they've read that they will never forget, to highlight the impact that certain books can have on them. (See Figure 4.2a–c.)

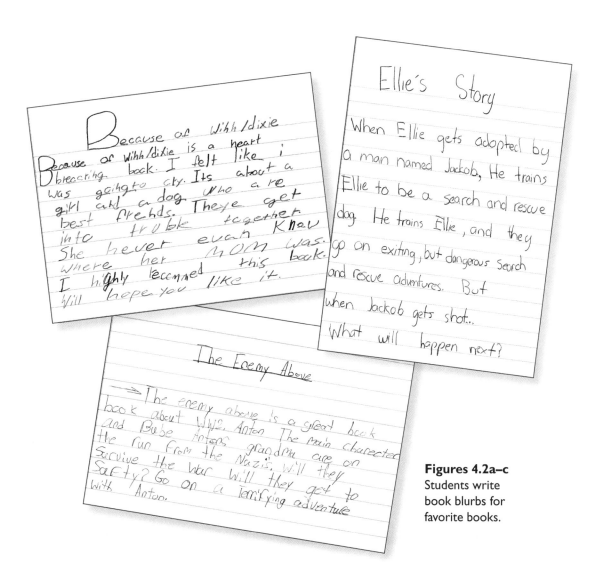

Figures 4.2a–c
Students write book blurbs for favorite books.

Increasing Awareness of Readership During Revision Work

The goals of the classroom press function as guidelines for students about what is and is not published in your classroom. Unlike their DIY books that aren't revised with an editor, the publications of your press aim to impact readers, causing readers to think and talk about the ideas represented by your press.

Even when students know the goals of the classroom press, they may lose track of these goals while writing. When you, as their editor, make sure students are familiar with what your press publishes, they will write with a greater sense of audience. Having a classroom press doesn't make for perfect rough drafts by any means, but it does ensure that students submit drafts that you care about and want to spend time revising. Just like authors in the "real world," your writers require and deserve the services of an editor to make their texts reach their readers. Through revision work, you can help students strengthen their texts to highlight their social purposes and have greater impact on readers.

When students submit their drafts, your goal will be to help them make their writing not only clear, but original and powerful. As you embed suggestions within the typed text, keep the reader in mind. Readers will turn away from texts that are rambling. Overly simplistic texts won't surprise or pique reader interest. Readers won't be satisfied by simplistic endings where a parent appears and solves the problem for the main character with a quick phone call to the principal. Adults can be allies in student stories, but passive kid characters should develop to take action. During revision, students can complicate their characters so they are not all good or all bad. As editors, we should take extra care to make sure our publications disrupt rather than perpetuate social stereotypes.

Ursula Nordstrom often wrote letters to her authors. She started her letters with the greeting, "Dear Genius." I've taken up this habit during the revision process. After I embed suggestions in a draft, I write a quick letter to the author that:

- highlights positive elements in the text

- points out the most essential revisions

- suggests how the reader will respond to the text

- encourages students to work on the revisions right away because we are eager to publish the manuscript.

We want our students to write texts that have impact, start some conversations, and are thought-provoking.

As students respond to revision suggestions, they see the power of revision to develop their ideas. They are motivated by revision rather than resistant to it when they feel supported by an editor as they change and improve their stories. Frances (Figure 4.3) took a while to land on a theme for her writing. After several starts, she decided to focus on bullying, a common theme for elementary school writers and a prominent theme in many of the books they read. Even when students explore the same theme, their stories will be original and represent a creative first for each writer.

Figure 4.3 Frances revises by adding dialogue and background information.

Frances was an active, spirited third grader who never backed down in arguments with others. In the first draft of her story, *Mac and the Bully*, Mac and Tyler don't get along. Tyler is new to the school. When Mac notices him bullying and threatening kids, he stands up to Tyler, pushing him to the ground. Mac gets in trouble with the principal, but eventually the principal sees that Tyler started the problems. Tyler is expelled at the end of the story. Problem solved.

On the plus side, Frances' story was unique in that both main characters act out physically and both get into trouble. I liked that her main character wasn't a pushover. Often students portray the bullied character as a sweet victim, all goodness and light.

I suggested to Frances that she dig a little deeper into the motivations for Tyler's aggression. Readers connect to a story when they understand a character's motivation. As Frances' editor, I wanted to help her communicate to readers that bullying is a complicated theme or issue. People usually don't bully for no reason at all. I shared an article about bullying with her when we met for a writing conference. The article listed reasons that kids bully other kids. I stapled the article to her typed draft. In my editor's letter to her, I wrote:

Dear Genius,

I love that both your characters have a problem with bullying. That's unusual in a book, and I think it's realistic. Your readers will be interested in your main character because he's complicated—not all good and not all bad. I've found some information about why people bully that could be worked into the story's ending. I think your characters should figure out a way to work out their problems without the principal's help. Please make revisions in the spaces I've left in your story. Great job with the manuscript so far! We are looking forward to publishing your story at Popcorn Press.

Sincerely,
Your Loyal Editor

When I asked Frances why Tyler was bullying people, she answered, "He likes his old school better. He doesn't like his new school."

"That makes sense. That needs to be clear in your story," I told her. "Your readers will learn that there are usually reasons behind a character's actions."

When Frances revised her story, she wanted readers to get to know the characters through dialogue and some background information (Figure 4.4).

In her published manuscript, Mac talks to Tyler and discovers that Tyler's upset about his move. Mac understands and reveals that he also has had to move to a new school in the past. At the end, Tyler and Mac become friends. Frances dedicated her book "to everyone who has experienced being bullied." In writing this book,

On Friday afternoon, Mac and Max found Tyler in the parking lot. He had a dodge ball in his hands. "I see you made it," said Tyler. "I wish you luck because we're playing dodge ball."

Max stood behind Mac. He was afraid. Mac stared Tyler right in the eyes and stood tall. "Why are you so angry, Tyler?" he said. "I liked my old school better than this dumb." he said. My dad wanted to move so I had to.

XXXX Maybe Tyler can tell Mac that he's mad that he had to change schools. Maybe he even had to leave his dog behind when they moved.

XXXX Maybe they can both decided that they're NOT going to hit each other. Maybe they can walk over to the ice cream shop together. "I know how you feel," said Mac. "Once I had to move. But now I love my school. I know you like ice cream to!" And they all went to get ice cream.

Figure 4.4 Frances' Revisions

she explored an important theme, revised to make her ending more realistic, and focused on kids as problem solvers.

Glenn (Figure 4.5) chose to write a story around the theme of friendship, but as he wrote his draft, he lost track of this theme. In his submitted manuscript, *The Hockey Game*, Dan is excited to play hockey. At the first practice of the season, a teammate pushes him and he breaks his arm. Dan has to sit out the rest of the season. The next season, Dan rejoins the team and wins the first game at the final buzzer by scoring a winning goal. In my editor's letter to Glenn, I wrote what appears at the top of the next page.

Dear Genius,

Great story! I can see that hockey is so important to Dan. The friendship theme needs to be strengthened before we can publish your story. Please look over my suggestions and work on the revisions SOON so we can bring your draft to the next step in the publishing process. I look forward to reading your next draft!

From,
Your Loyal Editor

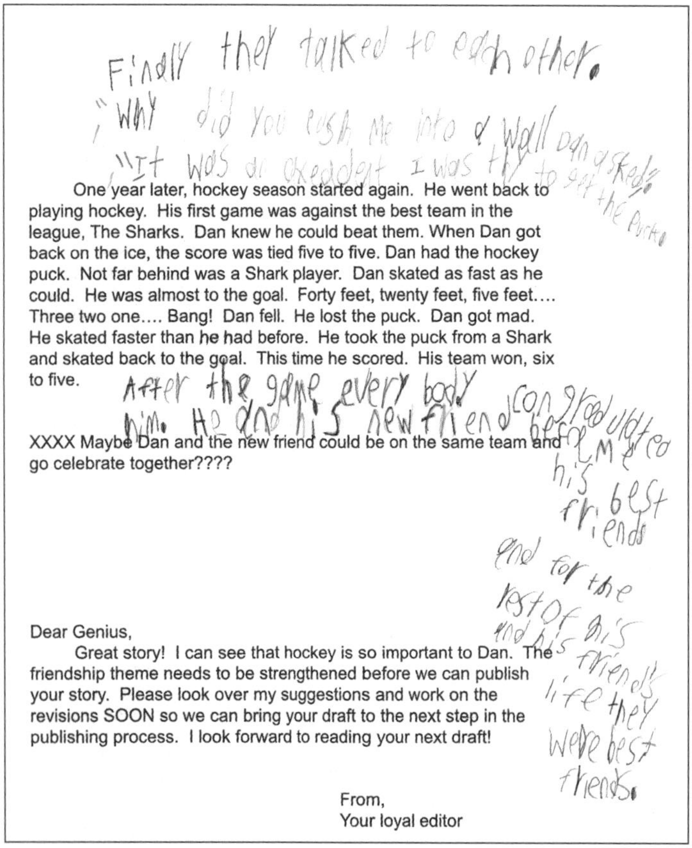

Finally they talked to each other.
"Why did you push me into a wall"
"It was an accadent. I was trying to get the puck"

One year later, hockey season started again. He went back to playing hockey. His first game was against the best team in the league, The Sharks. Dan knew he could beat them. When Dan got back on the ice, the score was tied five to five. Dan had the hockey puck. Not far behind was a Shark player. Dan skated as fast as he could. He was almost to the goal. Forty feet, twenty feet, five feet.... Three two one.... Bang! Dan fell. He lost the puck. Dan got mad. He skated faster than he had before. He took the puck from a Shark and skated back to the goal. This time he scored. His team won, six to five.

After the game every body congratulated him. He and his new friend

XXXX Maybe Dan and the new friend could be on the same team and go celebrate together????

could be his best friends and for the rest of his life they were best friends. life they were best friends.

Dear Genius,
    Great story! I can see that hockey is so important to Dan. The friendship theme needs to be strengthened before we can publish your story. Please look over my suggestions and work on the revisions SOON so we can bring your draft to the next step in the publishing process. I look forward to reading your next draft!

From,
Your loyal editor

Figure 4.5a Glenn's Revisions

When I met with Glenn, I asked him, "What happened to the friendship theme?"

"I decided I wanted to write a hockey story instead."

"I know you love hockey, but we publish books with social themes at Popcorn Press, so you're going to have to make some revisions before we can publish. I made some suggestions about the main character coming to be friends with the boy who pushed him. Look these over and let me know what you think."

I didn't abandon Glenn to figure out revisions on his own. I suggested ways he could develop his theme and then Glenn came up with some creative solutions within the text. As the editor of Popcorn Press, I keep in mind that our press has certain goals. Like the small presses mentioned earlier in this chapter, we aim to publish books that contribute to conversations about important issues in readers' lives. I could have let Glenn ignore his proposal goals, but that would have shown his readers that our press doesn't have a consistent identity, that we don't

Figure 4.5b After revisions are complete, Glenn works on illustrations.

stand for publishing books that can raise awareness of social themes.

I helped Glenn revise so the story was no longer about one kid winning a game, but a story that contributes to conversations about how even members of the same team can have disagreements and that people make mistakes but can talk through their problems and reconcile. While maintaining the spirit of his story, we strengthened the theme and integrated the idea of friendship into a story about Glenn's favorite sport. Glenn was happy with his published book about a character who scores the winning goal in a big hockey game, assisted by his new friend.

Eliot wanted to write about animal rights, a big topic for his class because of numerous discussions about articles in a newsmagazine for kids that the class receives regularly. Current events and morning meeting topics are often the source of topics for writers.

Eliot took writing seriously. His book, *Lost Dog*, is about two brothers whose dog gets lost. When his owners find him, they see some college students throwing rocks at him. The brothers bring the dog home and later join with a neighbor to form an animal rights club.

An avid college basketball fan, Eliot reported on our local team's scores daily at morning meeting. I was surprised that he had college kids mistreating a dog in his story and he told me that he had seen fans get very wild at games. "They even shout out swear words sometimes," he told me seriously.

I suggested that Eliot revise the mistreatment of the dog in his story. Rather than have the older students throwing rocks at the dog, I suggested that they spray paint the dog. "Maybe they're painting some signs about the big game, and the dog comes by, and they're just fooling around, but they spray some paint on the dog. I think throwing rocks at a dog is just too violent for your readers." Eliot agreed and made the revisions. He also added a detail about the animal club working at the local animal shelter. In my letter to Eliot, I wrote:

Dear Genius,

Great story with two strong themes—animal rights and friendship! I think the dog needs a name and a snapshot description. Your readers will like the ending where the kids start a club for animal rights. There are revision suggestions in the text, so please make changes soon. We want to publish your story!

Sincerely,
Your Loyal Editor

I marked my suggestions with X's and in this instance, I completely left this revision up to the writer. Although I suggested to Eliot that he add information about what the animal club might be reading about, I wrote, "Maybe mention three things they learned. Or not!" Eliot already had a powerful story that explored a social theme and showed kids taking action together. Eliot chose to revise his story to add one detail about an incident of animal abuse we had discussed in class (Figure 4.6).

Eliot's story was a creative first for him, and for our press, an original mix of his interests, life experiences, and social justice themes. He highlighted abuse of animals and showed that characters can work together to take realistic action. His readers will learn that animals are not always treated with care and that kids can take action to spread the word about animal rights.

Sometimes students want to write on a theme that we haven't studied in class. Anna wanted to write about homelessness. Her book, *Look Ahead of You*, tells the story about a family who experiences some financial problems and has to move out of their home. The main character, Mick, is an eleven-year-old girl who loves

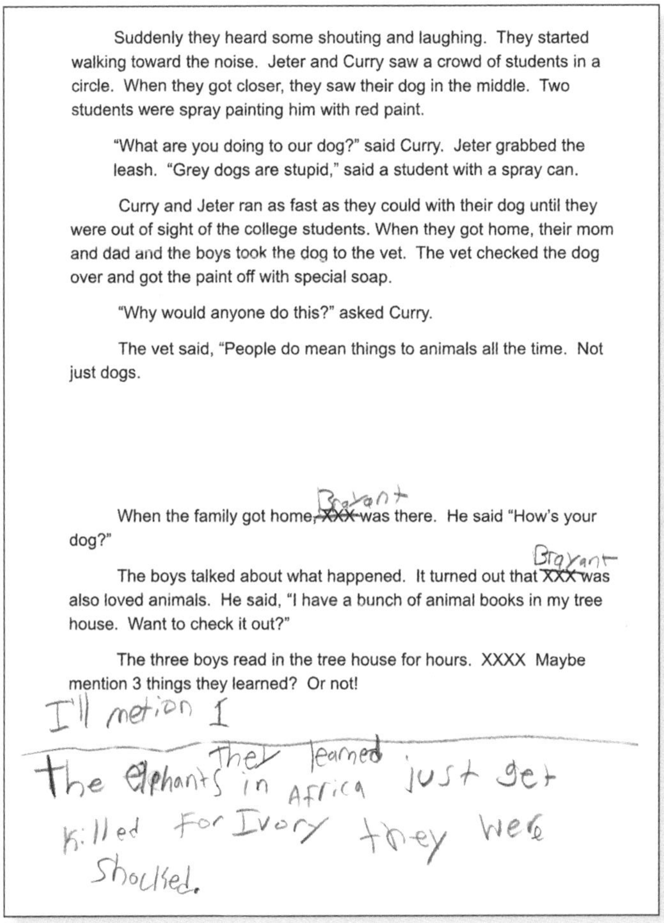

Suddenly they heard some shouting and laughing. They started walking toward the noise. Jeter and Curry saw a crowd of students in a circle. When they got closer, they saw their dog in the middle. Two students were spray painting him with red paint.

"What are you doing to our dog?" said Curry. Jeter grabbed the leash. "Grey dogs are stupid," said a student with a spray can.

Curry and Jeter ran as fast as they could with their dog until they were out of sight of the college students. When they got home, their mom and dad and the boys took the dog to the vet. The vet checked the dog over and got the paint off with special soap.

"Why would anyone do this?" asked Curry.

The vet said, "People do mean things to animals all the time. Not just dogs.

When the family got home, ~~XXX~~ Brayant was there. He said "How's your dog?"

The boys talked about what happened. It turned out that ~~XXX~~ Brayant was also loved animals. He said, "I have a bunch of animal books in my tree house. Want to check it out?"

The three boys read in the tree house for hours. XXXX Maybe mention 3 things they learned? Or not!

I'll metion I

They learned the elphants in Africa just get killed for Ivory they were shocked.

Figure 4.6 Eliot adds powerful details.

spending time with her best friend Kimmy. When Mick's family is suddenly homeless, they live on the streets. Mick gets a job to help out. The friendship comes to an abrupt end. Through our revision work, I shared with Anna some information from the Internet about homeless shelters and suggested that her characters move to a shelter for a short time. Because she was tackling a difficult social issue in her text, she owed it to her readers to do some research and to weave some information into her character's story. Our town has several housing options for homeless families, and I wanted Anna's story to show how important these options can be. I also suggested that after a few months, things might get better for the family and the two friends could be reunited. In her Dear Genius letter I wrote,

Dear Genius,

You have written a strong story here about the problems families face when they're homeless. I found some information about families living in shelters. Your readers might not realize that many towns have resources for homeless families. Read this over and let me know what you think about the family living in a shelter, rather than on the street. I hope you can bring Kimmy back into the ending of the story because she's so important to Mick at the beginning. Please work on these revisions as soon as possible because we are eager to publish your story at Popcorn Press!

From,
Your Loyal Editor

Anna read over my suggestions and revised to have her characters stay in a homeless shelter for a few months (Figure 4.7).

She also had Mick and Kimmy reunite in her story's new conclusion. Though Anna's story didn't connect with themes on our History Trail, she cared passionately about this issue. She dedicated her book to "everybody who is homeless. Always have hope." During our revision work, I gathered resources to help her research her topic. Her story was a creative first for our press and through the writing, we both learned more about an important social issue. Her book may inspire conversations about what happens to friendships when families fall on hard times.

Because of the Dear Genius letters and the revision suggestions embedded in the drafts, our conferences have clear direction during writing workshop (Figure 4.8). The workshop is still active and busy, but the time is more focused as students either can move forward with next steps for revision or talk to me about ideas for revisions if they're stuck or if they disagree with a suggestion.

building for a meeting, Mick sat down on a bench and stared at the cold scary world. She worried about what would happen. How would she get her homework? She saw a baby bird on a branch overhead. It was hopping from branch to branch. He kept trying to fly. Then he finally flew away. Mick knew she had to be brave. She looked up and saw a poster in a bakery window across the street. It said, "HIRING TODAY."

XXXX Maybe they could live at a homeless shelter for a few weeks? Check out the information below. I think that might be more common than the family living out on the streets????

When She walked in to the bakery. She saw a man sitting behind the lonely desk, playing a guitar.
"I'm here about the ad that's up," Mick said.
"Can you start on Wednesday?"
"Really? Thanks!" said Mick. "Thanks a lot."
Then she went back to the homeless shelter and got some soup and talked with other people.
was done
When she came out, she saw her parents. She told them about her new job. The news was overbearing for them. "I can't believe my eleven year old daughter has a job, and we don't," whispered her father. Her mom just gave him a sad look. They got their things out of the car and walked into the shelter together.

Figure 4.7 Anna revises to share information.

Figure 4.8 Students have revision suggestions in their texts, which gives clear direction to our writing conferences.

Marketing Student Writing

One summer morning, I visited my favorite local coffee shop. Before sitting down with my latte, I checked out the pamphlets and brochures on the shelf near the door. I picked up a small card, half the size of a business card, with a simple drawing of a dinosaur and a website address. I checked out the website and was delighted to find that this simple card led to information about two local authors and their self-published picture book. Dropping off these little cards was such a simple and clever way to market their writing. I started thinking about different ways to get the word out about writing in my classroom press.

All writers want readers. In writing workshop classrooms, writing is celebrated and shared at publishing parties (Figure 4.9) and proudly displayed in classroom libraries. In our small presses, students not only know the impact that writing can have on readers, but also can help market and distribute their texts to readers outside the classroom.

Figure 4.9 Publishing Party

Stephen Lloyd Webber's notion of "narrowcast marketing" is helpful to teachers who want to spread the word about classroom publication lists:

> Marketing is within reach of everyone who is passionate about the subject, style, or genre of writing, because to be successful, all you have to do is reach people directly based on a shared interest. You don't need to broadcast your message to the whole world. Instead, "Narrowcast" your message authentically to the right people (people like you), and you'll find an eager audience ready and waiting. . . .
>
> It's important simply to remember that marketing is a way of empowering ourselves to connect with other people. When you believe in what you're doing, it really is as simple as the desire to share something of value with others. (2013, 204–205)

Marketing our students' writing can range from bookmarks to blog posts. When we narrowcast information about our students' publications, we are showing them how to share their writing with a wider audience. When you publish class books, send sample copies to other classes in your school and in your district. If you have intraschool mail, you can pop student texts into school mail envelopes with a letter about your press. Include bookmarks that advertise your press. Students can also spread the word about your press by leaving these bookmarks at your school library's circulation desk (Figures 4.10a and 4.10b).

Figure 4.10a Students make simple bookmarks promoting our press for the school library's circulation desk.

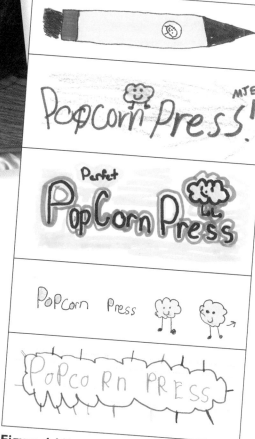

Figure 4.10b Bookmarks for the classroom press can be sent out to other classes or distributed from the school library circulation desk.

Invite other classes to send publications from their classrooms to you.

When students publish their own picture books, have them make two copies, one for their portfolios and one to use as part of your classroom library. Students can illustrate both texts lightly in pencil and then trace their drawings with black ink pen. These black-and-white pages can be put through the school copier and then students can color both copies.

Once the pages are colored, books can be bound simply by stapling the colored pages between colorful tagboard. Students add titles, author's notes, and dedications, using writing apps on their tablets or iPads or writing freehand. Use decorative duct tape for the spine on picture books. On the back of the book, students draw the logo for the classroom press, the final step on the publishing journey. Publications don't have to be fancy.

Keep a black-and-white master copy of an exceptionally powerful story for use with future classes. If a former student agrees, use their text to teach current students about the publishing process. In small groups, students can write book blurbs and color and bind these sample books to send off in school mail to other classes at your grade level in the district (Figure 4.11a). Include a class letter explaining the goals of your press (Figure 4.11b).

If your press has a web page, include the URL in your letter so that other students can visit. You don't need to have your entire class' stories on the web page. Each year, add one or two stories. Make sure to get parental permission for using student drafts

Figure 4.11a–b
Students can help send out sample classroom press publications to other classes or other schools.

on your web page. Parents are usually happy to have their child's story featured on the classroom press website.

You can also advertise your press at school with a bulletin board. Add a QR code for your web page and students can use their tablets to connect to the web page, read some sample stories from past years, and know about your classroom press. (See Figure 4.12.) Students around the building will come to know that your classroom is a publishing place. Other classrooms may start their own presses. Writers want their work to be read. Teacher–editors help with marketing because that's what a publishing house is all about—bringing books on a journey from a writer's first draft into the hands of readers.

When your classroom becomes a small press during writing workshop, student awareness of readership and audience increases naturally. As their editor, you can help students clarify, strengthen, and expand their writing purposes. While working with students to get their books into the hands of readers, the teacher–editor analyzes how student writing contributes to the ideas and conversations of our market audiences. We want to publish trendsetting writing, reaching out to readers inside and outside the classroom doors.

Figure 4.12 Advertise your press on hallway bulletin boards.

Frequently Asked Questions About the Classroom Press

5

Joshua was having trouble with his ending. "I don't know how to end this," he told me. "I don't like the ending I made on my storyboard."

We talked about the conflict and the main theme of his story. I suggested a possible ending, but Joshua shook his head. I thought for a moment and came up with another possibility. He shook his head again and said, "No, I don't want to write it like that."

"Well, endings can be hard. Maybe you can make a list of three possible endings and we can talk again after you've done some more thinking about it?"

As I got up to go, Joshua said, "But what other ideas do you have?"

I smiled and said, "Sorry, kiddo. That's all I've got for you today."

He looked indignant and shouted, "But you're my editor!"

I thought this was funny at first, but he had a point, so I regrouped. "Here's the thing, Joshua. I am your editor and I want to help you with your ending. But I've

given you several ideas. I think the last idea I talked about could work really well, but it's up to you to decide what to do next."

He thought a moment and said, "OK, I think I will try your idea."

Joshua wasn't crazy about my suggestions at first, but he changed his mind and went on to write a new ending to his story that we both agreed worked well.

I give suggestions freely to student writers now that I've taken up an editor mindset, but I'm also clear with students that having an editor does not mean that their teacher turns into a suggestion factory. Where I used to be timid to suggest specific ideas, now I jump in, knowing that the writer ultimately chooses to take up a suggestion or not.

The role of editor in the classroom press is based on the interactions of authors with editors in the world of publishing. The more I learn about how editors and authors work together, the more committed I become to the basic tenets of the teacher-as-editor stance. The positive response of my students and the quality of the work they produce also shore up my resolve to continue to develop and refine my editorial role during writing workshop. The classroom press writing workshop model is based on writing research and also offers practical guidelines from editors in the field of publishing. My own working relationships with editors on publishing projects, including the one that has resulted in this book, has reinforced my belief that our students deserve an editor's attention when they publish.

Editing student drafts is never going to be quick and easy work but it can go faster when we don't over-think and second-guess our place in the revision process. Working as a classroom press editor involves give-and-take with students, and we expect our students to significantly revise their work as we work together. When I've shared this work with colleagues and at conferences, I get asked certain questions again and again. Although there are no set procedures for revising student work and every publishing relationship is unique, keeping relationship, text, and readership in balance has helped to keep publishing projects positive and productive. I'm anticipating that readers of this book may well share a lot of these questions, so in this final chapter I'm going to address them.

FAQs About Fostering Relationships

How do students respond to having to revise so much in a classroom press?

For the most part, students enjoy getting their texts back, reading over suggestions, and seeing their texts change over time. It's not all smooth sailing, however, and every publishing project has its own tensions and its own ups and downs. I can help the tone stay upbeat by communicating to students that I am excited about their texts and pointing out the parts that stand out as strong.

Teachers know the value of strong relationships with students. We know that our students appreciate positive interest and support and tend to ignore negativity and nagging. When students feel their writing is valued and that I'm excited about how their drafts are progressing, they are more willing to have a go.

Sensitivity to a writer's reactions during the work pays off. Most students are pleased to work with an editor, but I've had moments when students reacted with resistance. Ashleigh was clearly annoyed when she read her typed draft and saw that I had not included her two pages of *very, very, very* in the

middle of her story. She said, "I want the *very* pages back in!" I told her that all her pages were still in her folder and she could use them for another piece of writing. I pointed out that she had a strong character and an important theme and that I believed that the dozens of *verys* were a distraction. I told her the lead had hooked me and I complimented her on creating a unique main character. She calmed down and we focused on the revision suggestions embedded in her story.

With older students, it's possible to be more direct and add some humor to revision conversations. A sixth-grade writer who wrote a fiction story with the theme of racism titled his story "The Racist Event." Every time I read it over, I typed different suggestions for new titles, asking tactfully, "What about a new title? This one doesn't draw me in to your great story." I expected him to change his title before publishing, but when he was working on illustrations for his book, I noticed a title page emerging from the printer that read, "The Racist Event" in large font. As the page clicked out of the printer, I blurted out, "Come on! What are you doing? That is *not* a good title!"

He burst out laughing and said, "I know! I can't think of anything! I've tried." Together we came up with a title from a key phrase in his story. This sixth grader knew that his title wasn't right and he good-naturedly agreed with my bold proclamation. My remark wasn't super sensitive, but this student handled it well. We had a positive relationship and had worked together on his story over several weeks. Most students truly appreciate revision help.

Is the classroom press editor similar to a coauthor?

An editor is not a coauthor. The editor and the author both contribute to the publication, but both have distinct roles and bring different perspectives to the work. The writer has to ultimately agree to suggestions and respond by creating new sections of text. Even though I freely give suggestions, student writers have agency about how they revise. When students get their drafts back, most eagerly read over suggestions. Some think awhile about how to respond and revise. Others feel a need to confer before they jump in. Still others reject suggestions and make a case for why their story works as it is.

When I worked with Ellie, she told me she did not like a suggestion I had made and she *really* did not want to incorporate it. Ellie wanted to have a lonely main character create a friend through her artwork. The main character draws a character in her sketchbook, who then comes to life. I thought the character could be an imaginary friend, but Ellie was adamant that she wanted this character to be real. I found her idea problematic because it seemed unusual that a kid would just appear and start living at a family's house, no questions asked, but together we came up with some background information about the new character that made sense for her to be part of the family. After we talked about this revision, Ellie was excited and wove the new story line into the text.

Revision work involves negotiation and give-and-take. When there's a section of the story that's stiff or confusing, disrupts the flow, or doesn't make sense in the world of that story (as was the case with Ellie), the editor must point this out to the writer, but the writer has to consent to and respond to suggestions. Though the work is interactive, the book is the author's accomplishment in the end. The publishing relationship can be described as a kind of symbiosis where the writer and editor both benefit. Both bring different things to the work and both get different things out of it.

What are the benefits of having a classroom press for students and teachers?

Students who write for a classroom press are guaranteed that their work will receive editorial attention and will be published. Our students don't receive the stack of rejection letters that are the bane of most authors. They're also not abandoned to revise on their own, without support. The work is not going to be easy, and one student did tell me that revision "can get on your nerves," but this statement shows that he was part of a true-to-life publishing project.

As a teacher, it's fun to be more involved in student writing projects and to help with changes to student texts. When a writer takes off running with revision suggestions, it's gratifying. We're not simply asking questions during conferences and crossing our fingers that students will follow through. When we suggest changes during writing conferences, we no longer cut our losses if students answer, "No thanks, I like it the way it is." Working together in our classroom presses, editors and writers feel pride in their texts and value the work that goes into revising and publishing.

FAQs About Improving Texts

How does a teacher–editor find the time to revise texts more than once?

Most of the stories described in this book are fiction stories, and we save those for the end of the year. During the first half of the school year, we work on shorter pieces, less than a page in length. Putting a limit on the length of rough drafts keeps the revision work more manageable. Shorter personal narratives or opinion pieces don't go through extensive revision. Every piece is revised, but not more than once or twice.

With fiction pieces, I focus on three to five manuscripts at a time. Students will be at different points in the writing and revision process. When students don't have a manuscript for the press to revise during a workshop session, they work on their own do-it-yourself books or write in their notebooks. They don't begin another piece for publication by our press.

We publish fewer texts, but spend more time on each publication. Working with student–authors, I'm always mindful of the issue of time. Sometimes the writers can get impatient toward the end and want the book to be finished before I consider it ready. The writers are usually quite surprised when their draft comes back to them because they haven't worked with an editor before. After a few exchanges, though, they get excited to see the ways their story develops as a result of revision.

Before I learned about editing, some students published more and some published less. Quick writers would publish eight to ten pieces a year, where others would publish three or four. With a classroom press, students publish the same amount, but the publishing is slowed down considerably. When students complete their books, they return to DIY publishing. The workshop comes to have a collective feel to it, with students helping each other, publishing less, but producing texts of higher quality.

Do students learn to revise on their own in a classroom press?

Using the revision template, kids practice revising in different ways. By editing in different colors, students read their text with varied aims. They read for potential meanings; elements of craft, social themes, and conventions; and spelling. The template functions as a formative assessment, allowing me to determine how to help students with their writing process.

Editors claim that they're not aiming to help a writer improve their writing skills. Instead, they help the writer revise to make their current book the best it can be. That's an emphasis on product that was missing from my writing workshop. By working with students to revise their drafts, rather than hoping that they'll do better next time, a classroom press editor makes sure that students experience the power of revision to improve texts. Students do become better revisers and indeed better writers during the school year, but regardless of this improvement, all students continue to receive revision assistance with their texts in a classroom press.

How do you make sure that you are true to the author's intentions for the text?

Editors read texts for what they could be, not what they are, but they are also respectful of the writer's intentions. Students list meanings that they think are important to their stories on the revision template. If students have problems filling out the template, we work together during a writing conference so I know what the writer is trying to get across to readers. As I read the text on my own, I keep these ideas in mind and look for ways to improve the text. I leave tracks in the text as I edit by typing questions or suggestions in italics and leaving spaces in the text where changes should be made. By using spaces and italics, I make sure my ideas about the text are distinct from the writer's draft. I also meet with students during writing conferences and talk with them about how their story is developing.

FAQs About Connecting with Readers

Who are the readers for classroom press publications?

There are many small presses in existence that are run by editors who make very little money from their work. Some make no money at all, but these editors want to help get writing that aligns with certain social goals out into the world. Small press editors are passionate about getting authors' work into the hands of readers. They publish writing online, present public readings for authors, and leave bookmarks and flyers around town for their presses. That kind of commitment to connecting writers with readers inspires me in my classroom. Popcorn Press books provide reading material for my classroom library. Student publications are not used merely for leisure reading, but as mentor texts for future writers. Students see that Popcorn Press texts stay in print and become part of the writing program for future writers. We also send samples from our texts out to other classes in our school and district. Sometimes we get writing back from these classes. The classroom press editor doesn't need to make sure their texts turn a profit, but increasing readership shows students that you are invested in their writing.

How do parents react to the classroom press?

Parents give rave reviews. When I first started taking on an editor stance, I was experimenting with the model, passing the writing back and forth, trying to figure out how to offer more suggestions without overtaking student stories. That first year, a student's father came and talked to me after we sent home published books in student portfolios. He didn't believe that his daughter had written her book. I showed him the multiple drafts in her writing folder and told him that we had passed the draft back and forth several times. He was thrilled to see the work she had put into her story.

I communicate with parents in my newsletters about the classroom press work we are doing. I also started teaching students more about the publishing process. Now, when they share their texts with their parents, they can explain the back-and-forth of the revision process. Over the years I've had many parents thank me for this work. They are happy to see their kids revising more and producing better writing.

FAQs About My Own Publishing Experiences

I tell students that I know that authors revise *a lot* before their text is published and I know *for a fact* that an editor is extremely involved with revision because I worked with an editor for several years to publish this book. As my editor, Holly, and I passed this book back and forth, I took her suggestions seriously

because she wasn't offering feedback for the fun of it. It was clear that she spent a lot of time reading each draft. Her suggestions were marked in different text colors or typed as margin notes, so she left tracks as editors do.

Like the editors I read about, Holly was committed to our relationship and valued my opinions. She would check in with me during the revision process asking me often, "What do you think?" or "I hope this captures what you want to say," when she made suggestions. Writing is emotional work, and I did feel anxious many times during the revision process, but I also experienced many moments of satisfaction and excitement as the book took shape over time. Working with Holly showed me the importance of checking in with writers along the way and not rushing into publication before a text is ready.

As editors do, Holly also kept readers in mind constantly during the work. She reminded me from day one to think about my audience. She challenged me to "think about your audience of teachers. Show them you understand what it's like to be frustrated by the kind of revision work students do and offer an alternative. . . . Give readers something specific they might try that day." She asked me to consider what readers would learn from my book and how they could apply that learning in their own classrooms. Through our emails and phone calls, we frequently discussed the purpose of this book and how the classroom press model might appeal to future readers.

In preparation for writing this final chapter, I reviewed three years of back-and-forth emails between Holly and me. I saved over fifty email strands concerning multiple revisions. Holly and I shared ideas not only through emails, but in numerous margin notes on each chapter and during phone calls. The following email from Holly is typical of her feedback over the years.

> *Thanks so much for sending this chapter. Your voice came through as gentle, reflective and knowledgeable—a nice combination for the reader. I'm completely engaged by your stories about author/editor relationships. It's clear how you transition from those stories to classroom applications, but it might*

need more direction for the reader. In the second half of the chapter I offer suggestions for how you might lay out the practical, "how-to," pieces and weave in some of your great student writing samples. Do you think it's possible to send a revised chapter in the next few weeks? Let me know and let's schedule a time to talk if you think that'll help!

Holly made countless suggestions that helped guide the revisions of this book. Throughout the work, she offered encouragement and was always available to answer questions through email or on the phone. She kept future readers in mind and frequently pointed out ways to strengthen and clarify ideas. It sometimes made me nervous to share ideas about how editors work with my actual editor, but as our work progressed, I enjoyed seeing the three editor commitments coming to life as Holly and I traded the work back and forth during its publication journey.

While I share my own publishing experiences with students, they also become familiar with stories of their favorite authors working with their editors. Toward the end of a recent school year, our school benefitted from an author visit. Author and illustrator Kevin Hawkes was a charming presenter, and the kids were enthralled by his presentation. About halfway through his talk, he told the kids about an interaction with his editor, who once made a suggestion that he change one of his favorite illustrations. Hawkes was annoyed because he liked his illustration the way it was. He later thought about the suggestion and decided the editor was right. He made the change. More than 100 students were listening to Kevin, but at that moment the kids in my class swiveled their heads toward me, nodding and smiling, some even giving me thumbs up signs. A boy sitting next to me whispered, "We know about this! This is what we talk about!"

Kevin Hawkes wanted students to know that writers work with editors and that sometimes they make changes based on an editor's opinions

and ideas. It's an essential part of being a published author. When I first started working with students using a small press model, I often worried about crossing the line with my student writers. But editors must be bold. I now know that authors rely on their editors to make brave suggestions during the publication journey, and editors rely on the creativity of writers to produce the writing that eventually results in published books and stories.

As our students move from grade to grade, publishing for new classroom presses, they will develop new editor–author relationships, gain confidence in their ability to revise their texts, and learn how to connect with future readers through their writing. As classroom press editors, we learn on the job, developing our publishing houses each year as new writers with new stories enter our classrooms.

WORKS CITED

PROFESSIONAL BOOKS

Anderson, Carl. 2000. *How's It Going? A Practical Guide to Conferring with Student Writers*. Portsmouth, NH: Heinemann.

Anderson, Susan Heller. 1988. "Ursula Nordstrom, 78, a Nurturer of Authors for Children, Is Dead." *New York Times*, October 12. www.nytimes.com/1988/10/12/obituaries/ursula-nordstrom-78-a-nurturer-of-authors-for-children-is-dead.html.

Berlin, James. 1993. "Literacy, Pedagogy, and English Studies: Postmodern Connections." In *Critical Literacy: Politics, Praxis, and the Postmodern*, edited by Colin Lankshear and Peter McLaren, 247–70. Albany, NY: State University of New York Press.

Bird, Elizabeth. 2013. "Meet the Latest Newbery Winner: How Katherine Applegate Created a Modern-Day Classic." *School Library Journal* 3 (March 1). www.slj.com/2013/03/interviews/the-one-and-only-how-katherine-applegate-created-a-classic-and-nabbed-the-newbery/.

Bomer, Randy, and Katherine Bomer. 2002. *For a Better World: Reading and Writing for Social Action*. Portsmouth, NH: Heinemann.

Boushey, Gail, and Joan Moser. 2014. *The Daily 5: Fostering Literacy in the Elementary Grades*, 2nd ed. York, ME: Stenhouse.

Burke, James Lee. 2015. "About James Lee Burke." http://jamesleeburke.com/about-the-author/faq-for-jlb/#faq_16.

Calkins, Lucy. 1994. *The Art of Teaching Writing*. New edition. Portsmouth, NH: Heinemann.

Clifford, John, and Elizabeth Ervin. 1999. "The Ethics of Process." In *Post-Process Theory: Beyond the Writing-Process Paradigm*, edited by Thomas Kent, 179–97. Carbondale, IL: Southern Illinois University Press.

Curtis, Christopher, and Wendy Lamb. n.d. "Author–Editor Dialogues: Christopher Paul Curtis and Wendy Lamb." *CBC Magazine: The Children's Book Council*. Accessed August 25, 2007. www.cbcbooks.org/cbcmagazine/dialogues/www.cbcbooks.org/?s=Christopher+Paul+Curtis+and+Wendy+Lamb&submit.x=0&submit.y=0

Curtis, Richard. 1993. "Are Editors Necessary?" In *Editors on Editing: What Writers Need to Know About What Editors Do*, edited by Gerald Gross, 29–39. New York: Grove Press.

Elleman, Barbara. 1999. *Tomie dePaola: His Art and His Stories*. New York: G. P. Putnam's Sons.

Fogelman, Phyllis. 1993. "Editing Children's Books." In *Editors on Editing: What Writers Need to Know About What Editors Do*, edited by Gerald Gross, 304–14. New York: Grove Press.

Friedman, Fredrica. 1993. "On Editing Nonfiction: Multiple Majors in a University of Subjects." In *Editors on Editing: What Writers Need to Know About What Editors Do*, edited by Gerald Gross, 280–89. New York: Grove Press.

Graves, Donald. 1994. *A Fresh Look at Writing*. Portsmouth, NH: Heinemann.

Green, John. 2011. "Men Running on Tanks and the Truth About Book Editors." Vlogbrothers Vlog, June 6. https://youtu.be/oLwJT-HhhB0.

Gross, Gerald. 1993. Preface: "Reflections on a Lifetime of Editing." In *Editors on Editing: What Writers Need to Know About What Editors Do*, edited by Gerald Gross, xiii–xx. New York: Grove Press.

Haar, Catherine, and Alice Horning. 2006. "Introduction and Overview." In *Revision: History, Theory, and Practice*, edited by Alice Horning and Anne Becker, 4–9. W. Lafayette, IN: Parlor Press.

Hardin, Joe. 2001. *Opening Spaces: Critical Pedagogy and Resistance Theory in Composition*. New York: State University of New York Press.

HarperCollinsPublishers. 2017. "How a Book Is Made" web sampler. https://www.harpercollins.com/web-sampler/9780064460859.

Harste, Jerome, and Vivian Vasquez. 1998. "The Work We Do: Journal as Audit Trail." *Language Arts* 75 (4): 266–76.

Heffernan, Lee. 2004. *Critical Literacy and Writer's Workshop: Bringing Purpose and Passion to Student Writing*. Newark, DE: International Reading Association.

Heffernan, Lee, and Mitzi Lewison. 2003. "Social Narrative Writing: (Re)constructing Kid Culture in the Writer's Workshop." *Language Arts* 80 (6): 435–43.

Howard, Gerald. 1993. "Mistah Perkins—He Dead: Publishing Today." In *Editors on Editing: What Writers Need to Know About What Editors Do*, edited by Gerald Gross, 56–72. New York: Grove Press.

Hulbert, Ann. 1994. "Roald the Rotten." *New York Times Book Review*. Accessed April 26, 2015. www.nytimes.com/1994/05/01/books/roald-the-rotten.html.

Kamler, Barbara. 2001. *Relocating the Personal: A Critical Writing Pedagogy*. Albany, NY: State University of New York Press.

Lane, Barry. 1993. *After* The End: *Teaching and Learning Creative Revision*. Portsmouth, NH: Heinemann.

Lensmire, Timothy. 2000. *Powerful Writing, Responsible Teaching*. New York: Teachers College Press.

Lerner, Betsy. 2000. *The Forest for the Trees: An Editor's Advice to Writers*. New York: Riverhead Books.

Marcus, Leonard, ed. 1998. *Dear Genius: The Letters of Ursula Nordstrom*. New York: HarperCollins.

Oliver, Lauren. 2012. *How a Book Is Made*. Episode 3: "Editing the Book." Online Video Series. HarperCollins. www.wheredobookscomefrom.com

O'Shea Wade, James. 1993. "Doing Good—and Doing It Right." In *Editors on Editing: What Writers Need to Know About What Editors Do*, edited by Gerald Gross, 73–82. New York: Grove Press.

Pope, Alice, ed. 2005. *2006 Children's Writer's and Illustrator's Market: Where and How to Sell Your Children's Stories and Illustrations*. Cincinnati, OH: Writer's Digest Books.

Routman, Regie. 2000. *Conversations: Strategies for Teaching, Learning, and Evaluating*. Portsmouth, NH: Heinemann.

Sale, Faith. 1993. "Editing Fiction as an Act of Love." In *Editors on Editing: What Writers Need to Know About What Editors Do*, edited by Gerald Gross, 267–80. New York: Grove Press.

Schappell, Elissa. 1993. "Toni Morrison, the Art of Fiction No. 134." *The Paris Review* 128 (fall). www.theparisreview.org/interviews/1888/the-art-of-fiction-no-134-toni-morrison.

Scholastic. n.d. Flashling Readers. "See This Story Grow." www.scholastic.com/teachers/sites/default/files/asset/file/winndixie_story.pdf.

Schuster, M. Lincoln. 1993. "An Open Letter to a Would-Be Editor." In *Editors on Editing: What Writers Need to Know About What Editors Do*, edited by Gerald Gross, 22–27. New York: Grove Press.

Sendak, Maurice. 1990. "Visitors from My Boyhood." In *Worlds of Childhood: The Art and Craft of Writing for Children*, edited by William Zinsser, 47–70. Boston: Houghton Mifflin.

Shor, Ira. 1999. "What Is Critical Literacy?" In *Critical Literacy in Action: Writing Words, Changing Worlds*, edited by Ira Shor and Caroline Pari, 1–30. Portsmouth, NH: Heinemann.

Silbersack, John. 1993. "Editing the Science-Fiction and Fantasy Novel: The Importance of Calling Everyone Fred." In *Editors on Editing: What Writers Need to Know About What Editors Do*, edited by Gerald Gross, 290–303. New York: Grove Press.

SooHoo, Suzanne, and Brenda Brown. 1994. "Developing Voice in the Democratic Classroom." In *If This Is Social Studies, Why Isn't It Boring?*, edited by Stephanie Steffey and Wendy J. Hood, 97–106. York, ME: Stenhouse.

The Telegraph. 2010. "Hand-written JK Rowling Manuscripts to Go on Display," September 19. www.telegraph.co.uk/culture/books/booknews/8012289/Hand-written-JK -Rowling-manuscripts-to-go-on-display.html.

Tobin, Lad. 1993. *Writing Relationships: What Really Happens in the Composition Class*. Portsmouth, NH: Boynton/Cook–Heinemann.

Treglown, Jeremy. 1994. *Roald Dahl: A Biography*. London: Faber and Faber.

Waxman, Maron. 1993. "Line Editing: Drawing Out the Best Book Possible." In *Editors on Editing: What Writers Need to Know About What Editors Do*, edited by Gerald Gross, 153–69. New York: Grove Press.

Webber, Stephen Lloyd. 2013. *Writing from the Inside Out: The Practice of Free-Form Writing*. Studio City, CA: Divine Arts.

Welch, Nancy. 1997. *Getting Restless: Rethinking Revision in Writing Instruction*. Portsmouth, NH: Heinemann.

Williams, Alan D. 1993. "What Is an Editor?" In *Editors on Editing: What Writers Need to Know About What Editors Do*, edited by Gerald Gross, 3–9. New York: Grove Press.

Yolen, Jane. 2003. *Take Joy: A Book for Writers*. Cincinnati, OH: Writer's Digest Press.

CHILDREN'S LITERATURE

Aliki. 1988. *How a Book Is Made*. New York: HarperCollins.

Applegate, Katherine. 2012. *The One and Only Ivan*. New York: HarperCollins.

Browne, Anthony. 1998. *Voices in the Park*. New York: Dorling Kindersley.

Bunting, Eve. 2001. *Gleam and Glow*. Illustrated by Peter Sylvada. New York: Harcourt.

Cameron, W. Bruce. 2015. *Ellie's Story*. New York: Starscape.

Clements, Andrew. 2001. *The School Story*. New York: Atheneum Books.

Cremin, Peadar. 2002. "Fight for Child Workers!" In *Rethinking Globalization: Teaching for Justice in an Unjust World*, edited by Bill Bigelow and Bob Peterson, 206–207. Portland, OR: Rethinking Schools.

DiCamillo, Kate. 2015. *Because of Winn-Dixie*. Somerville, MA: Candlewick.

Haddix, Margaret Peterson. 2001. *The Girl with 500 Middle Names*. London, UK: Aladdin.

Krull, Kathleen. 2003. *Harvesting Hope: The Story of Cesar Chavez*. Illustrated by Yuyi Morales. New York: Harcourt.

Lester, Julius. 2000. *To Be a Slave*. Illustrated by Tom Feelings. New York: Puffin.

McCully, Emily Arnold. 1996. *The Bobbin Girl*. New York: Dial.

Nieves, Augustino. 2002. "Child Labor Is Cheap—and Deadly: The Testimony of Augustino Nieves." In *Rethinking Globalization: Teaching for Justice in an Unjust World*, edited by Bill Bigelow and Bob Peterson, 204–207. Portland, OR: Rethinking Schools.

Oliver, Lauren. 2013. *The Spindlers*. New York: HarperCollins.

Parker, David L. 2002. *By These Hands: Portraits from the Factory Floor*. St. Paul: Minnesota Historical Society Press.

Rowling, J. K. 1997. *Harry Potter and the Philosopher's Stone*. London, UK: Bloomsbury.

Sendak, Maurice. 1963. *Where the Wild Things Are*. New York: HarperCollins.

Shea, Pegi Dietz. 2003. *The Carpet Boy's Gift*. Illustrated by Leane Morin. Gardiner, ME: Tilbury House.

Silverstein, Shel. 1964. *The Giving Tree*. New York: HarperCollins.

Spradlin, Michael. 2016. *The Enemy Above: A Novel of World War II*. New York: Scholastic.

White, E. B. 1952. *Charlotte's Web*. Illustrated by Garth Williams. New York: Harper Brothers.

Yashima, Taro. 1976. *Crow Boy*. New York: Puffin.

Yin. 2001. *Coolies*. Illustrated by Chris Soentpiet. New York: Puffin.

Zolotow, Charlotte. 1972. *William's Doll*. New York: Harper and Row.

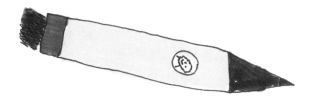